Love Beyond Death

A Remarkable Account
of a Journey into
Other realms

Love Beyond Death

A Remarkable Account
of a Journey into
Other realms

Elleke van Kraalingen

BOOKS

Winchester, UK
Washington, USA

First published by O-Books, 2011
O-Books is an imprint of John Hunt Publishing Ltd., The Bothy, Deershot Lodge, Park Lane, Ropley, Hants, SO24 0BE, UK
office1@o-books.net
www.o-books.com

For distributor details and how to order please visit the 'Ordering' section on our website.

ISBN: 978 1 84694 379 9

A CIP catalogue record for this book is available from the British Library.

Design: Stuart Davies

Printed in the UK by CPI Antony Rowe
Printed in the USA by Offset Paperback Mfrs, Inc

CONTENTS

For each of us - perhaps once or twice only in the whole course of our life - there have been sudden moments of discovery when we have seen disclosed the deepest being and truth of another, and we have experienced his or her inner life as if it were our own, and this encounter with the true personhood of another is, once more, a contact with the transcendent and timeless, with something stronger than death.
To say to another, with all our heart, 'I love you', is to say,
'You will never die'.
Bishop Kallistos of Dioklea
*In: The Wedding Present**

Every experience of love gives us yet another glimpse of the meaning of love in God himself.
Human love is the instrument we can use to explore the mystery of love which God is.
Human love reflects divine love and, indeed, transmits it.
Basil Hume
*In: The Wedding Present**

Foreword

This is a most remarkable document. It details how, out of the most terrible tragedy, came a series of experiences that not only add to the evidence for survival of physical death, but present us with accounts of mystical experiences offering insights into rarefied dimensions of being. After many years of studying psychical research and meeting with first-hand psychic experiences of my own, I have to say that it breaks new and exciting ground in the subject, and leaves the reader feeling uplifted and deeply moved. In addition to its other qualities, it offers us a love story that transcends physical death, and reassures us that ultimately love triumphs over the separation of death.

I am in the fortunate position of having met the author, and of conducting several long conversations with her about her experiences. She is woman of great integrity who knows what she experienced, and the life-changing consequences for her that resulted. As a qualified and experienced psychologist, Elleke is well aware of the possibility that the trauma of the tragedy that preceded her experiences somehow unsettled her grasp on reality, and she is able for good reasons to reject this possibility. We as readers must be careful not to try and 'explain away' her experiences in order to make them fit into some materialistic framework, a favourite trick of the rational mind that all too often seeks to strip life of any meaning beyond that provided by the material world. The rational mind, for all its competence in relating to outer reality, persists in trying to intrude into those areas of inner experience of which it has no knowledge and about which it has nothing to say, and attempting to dismiss them as nothing more than psychological aberrations. Of course, the reader must ultimately make up his or her own mind as to what happened to Elleke, but for myself I am satisfied that the account she gives of her experiences faithfully portrays genuine and deeply spiritual events.

Mercifully, tragedies such as that experienced by Elleke are rare, but they do occur, and the reader may wonder why others who go through their own tragedies are not given similar reassurances that life is eternal. There are several possible answers. Many of the abruptly bereaved may indeed go through something comparable to Elleke, but may keep their experiences to themselves, either through fear of ridicule or because the experiences are too intensely personal to share. Another possibility is that would-be communicator may lack the psychic or spiritual facilities to make contact. Similarly the recipient of the experiences may lack the facilities necessary to receive the contacts, or to bear the physical and psychological strains involved (the demands upon Elleke's health were extreme). And no matter how close the relationship between communicator and recipient, the particular kind of spiritual alchemy necessary for contact to be established may not be present. Finally, we must not forget that there are other less overwhelming ways in which the deceased may make their presence felt. We have evidence that although over 40 per cent of bereaved spouses or partners sampled by researchers report some kind of contact with the deceased, these typically take the form of an awareness of an unseen presence, or of the scent of the deceased's familiar perfume, or of the repeated and inexplicable movement of household objects owned by the deceased, experiences that are easier for the bereaved to handle and that make less demands upon them than those met with by Elleke.

In spite of these demands, was Elleke privileged to have the life-changing experiences vouchsafed to her? Undoubtedly she was, and all credit must go to her not only for sustaining the extreme demands that they made of her, but on having the ability to view them so perceptively, and to describe them to us in such detail. For these reasons and for the rarity of the experiences and for all the many lessons they have to teach us, her book deserves to become a classic in the literature on survival of physical death.

It allows us to recognise that such extraordinary events are possible, and it consequently widens our horizons of understanding in so many ways. It adds significantly to our knowledge of post-mortem possibilities, and provides valuable lessons on the nature of the afterlife and on the more exalted levels of mystical experience. Above all perhaps, it teaches us the triumph of love, not only of love between two people, but of the love that lies at the centre of existence and provides existence with meaning and spiritual purpose. A life-enhancing book that will enrich all those who read it.

Professor David Fontana FBPsS,
Former President Society for Psychical Research

Preface

This is my story, based on my own experiences. I have written it, because I couldn't do otherwise.

I wrote for myself, for Hermod, for the people around us and anyone else, to whom it can be of any value. For in life we all live our own story and we enrich ourselves through listening to each other's stories.

The dialogues are repeated verbatim, as far as my memory has permitted, supported by extracts from my diaries.

For a long time I wondered whether to make a story of it, in which the experiences would happen to fictitious other persons. This seemed safer, but I have decided that it will be simply my story, without making it appear more or less than what it is. It is my version of my reality.

The persons mentioned in this story, have given their permission in trust, without prior knowledge of what has been written. They are by no means responsible for what follows. Everyone may think of it as they wish.

Elleke

1

On the way to Paradise

An inner thread
of a secret tapestry
linking our souls together

Love unfolding
trust developing
growing
towards, into, within
each other
radiating out
into the world

One more step
on the way to paradise

Schiphol, February

Tap, tap, tap, tap, tap........ My heels are tapping on the stone tiles as I hurry through the passage to the gate. It sounds ladylike, too ladylike. Maybe I am not wearing the right shoes for a tropical dream trip after all. And my haste does not fit either, but as usual I have arrived at the airport just in time for check-in. Then I want to buy sun cream at my favourite body shop.

With all those extensions at Schiphol, the journey to the gates becomes longer and longer. One really has to allow extra time for the walk to the gate. There I am, at the departure gate for my flight to London. The waiting room is still full. The flight is not delayed, is it? Yes. Shit! A delay is showing of unknown duration. The plane has not arrived yet.

There is nothing to be done about it. I look around and see

how the people are sitting, standing and waiting uncomplainingly. Then my haste falls away. I find a place near a window and stare out. It is grey and rainy winter in the Dutch way.

Now he has to wait even longer for me in London. But anyhow, how often have I had to wait for him?

Inwardly smiling I remember the first time he came to visit me, when he was in Holland to attend a conference. This was a year and a half after our first meeting. Every quarter of an hour he phoned to say that he was a bit delayed, for yet again something had come up. Apparently he was as nervous as I was. During that year and a half we had got to know each other very well over the phone and had built a special friendship. Sparkling conversations lasting for hours were not exceptional and the distance from Norway to Holland did not exist over the phone.

Both of us were filled with contradictory feelings about this coming meeting, anticipation, expectation, attraction and doubts. Expectation because we had come so close to each other that we knew it would be good to see each other again, possibly more than good. The attraction had been clearly tangible over the phone. Remarkable how one can sense someone's essence through a piece of technology. The doubts rising from the delicacy of the situation.

After ten harmonious years my relationship had just broken down quite suddenly and I was now living alone with my three children. I felt very vulnerable in this situation. Over the phone he had made clear to me that he only came in friendship. He definitely did not intend to start a relationship with a woman with three children, although he admitted to having more than feelings of friendship towards me, which was mutual.

However from the very moment that he – finally - stood in front of my door, he melted. I saw it in his eyes. His intention to keep an amicable distance did not show any more. At first I was confused. He was so tall, taller than in my memory, so self-assured and overwhelming. Then I melted too, completely. We spent wonderful days together. It was as if we had always been together.

Later he said about this: "So this is how it can be between two people. I had always hoped it could be like this. Now it has come true."

Later, the first time I went to Norway, he came to fetch me from the airport an hour too late, because he had not finished clearing up his apartment. He had been busy with this for weeks. The next time he came to stay with me and the children, he had forgotten to confirm his booking, so he had to come two days later. Then he forgot his passport and again he had to take another plane.

Curious lapses for an experienced traveller like he is, who had taken a three year trip round the world, and these days is constantly on the road. Last summer he missed the night train from Copenhagen. And last autumn he planned to come by car and ferry and became ill on the day of departure and had to postpone it by another day. Then last Christmas I was waiting in the snow with my luggage at a small Norwegian railway station, for some time before he dashingly arrived to pick me up.

Timelessness was something I had to accept in this man if I wanted to be with him. But he always came. And he was endearing in his apologies and embarrassment about this irritating habit.

Nevertheless it is not surprising that I can hardly believe he really will be waiting for me this time at the end of the gate in London and that he won't have missed his plane again. No, he can wait a while for me now, so that he can feel how it is.

I walk up and down and observe the stoical faces around me. Everyone is caught up in their own thoughts, seemingly indifferent to their surroundings. I see my appearance reflected in the window. I'm still quite content with my outfit. A small black tricot dress with a golden-brown coloured shawl, with a black body-suit and black tights underneath and the black shoes with the tapping heels. The whole appearance is appropriate for the visit to his friends in London tonight, smart and neat, maybe even elegant, without extravagance.

On the long flight tomorrow it will fit easily and once I arrive in Jamaica I will put the body suit and the tights into my bag, not to take them out again until the journey home. And those shoes, well, they may be suitable for the conference, which we will be attending in the first week. I have some sandals and leather slippers in my travel bag.

The waiting crowd starts to move. The plane has arrived and is starting to board for the departure flight.

I am coming, my love. I shall be in your arms within little more than an hour.

In the plane, comfortably curled up in the seat, I am really starting to enjoy myself. I ignore the safety instructions by the stewards and withdraw inside myself. The travel bug attacks. It is lovely to be en route again! Especially such a dream trip as this, which I have been looking forward to for so long. Last year I got a ticket to any desired destination as a present from my mother for the completion of my psychology studies. However I was still too busy finding a new rhythm in life, at the time, alone with the children. Besides I had just got a new job. I did not have the energy for a trip and did not want to leave the children either.

Now it is different. I have found quite a good balance with the children by working within their school hours and being home for them in the afternoons. It has not been an easy year, though it was a good one. The children are doing fine and at home it is pleasant to be together. I am enjoying my work and there are good friends around me. And of course there is this new flourishing love.

It is the ideal time to use the ticket for the realization of a childhood dream. I call it my tropical-dream. The longing for a symbolic paradise. Swimming, playing and diving into the blue ocean, nourished by the sun, meditating on a white beach under a palm tree and finding a pearl.

This pearl is an inner pearl. I do not exactly know what it is about. It is a feeling that I am almost ready for something, though not entirely ready. It has to do with finding a point of silence within, an inner freedom. It is about letting go of fears and daring to be. Of course this pearl is not dependent upon a tropical paradise. It can be found at home on the couch as well, but an ideal environment might stimulate the opening up of something living inside.

In any case I believe that it is healthy to fulfill one's dreams. And after this last period I am ready to take some distance from my normal life and do something extravagant. Now I am able to leave with confidence. Peter, my ex-partner, is willing to be with the children for these weeks, and he is looking forward to it, as are the children. So I gratefully make use of this present from my mother. It really is a wonderful gift.

I feel there is a pearl to be found in my new relationship. During the past year and a half we have grown towards each other and now we are at the point of making a leap together. This has not been without a struggle. I think by definition it is not easy to have a relationship with someone based abroad. Jokingly I sometimes call it a telephone-relationship, or even an answering machine-relationship. Although this also has its charms. Wishing good night in the evening, or good morning in the morning, a sweet message on the answering machine, or long talks lasting hours at night. Almost daily we have shared everything, joy and sorrow.

Maybe just this physical distance has enabled us to come together. For I have clearly needed space in order to regain balance within myself and in life in general. And he needed the space to get used to the idea that he possibly will commit himself to a woman, especially a woman with three children.

He never made a secret of the fact that for his whole life he has had difficulty with commitment: not in friendships, he has beautiful friendships, the difficulty lies in intimate relationships. From the beginning of our relationship he has told me he has never been able to commit himself before and that possibly he would never be able to commit, especially not to someone with children. Although he is very fond of children, he has been frightened of the responsibility and the complexity of committing to four relationships at once. Which is hardly surprising. Because of his hesitation I have felt a bit uncertain as well. The only certainty I have is that I love him, unconditionally. He is the most beautiful and most difficult man I have ever met. And it is clear that he loves me too, even though it is not clear yet how we can shape a future together.

Some time ago I had decided to go for what I find essential in life. I find love essential. In love one can transcend oneself. Love is life, whether it be for children, family and friends, people around, love for beauty, for nature... or for a lover. Life is a lesson in love.

From the beginning there was love between us, but it took a little while before we dared to allow it.

The first night we were together he said, from the core of his heart: "I feel you everywhere inside and around me... but, that means that I'm also inside and around you!"

I could only agree with that.

"Pinch my arm, "he said.

"What?"

"Pinch my arm!"

"eh?"

"Otherwise I can't believe this is true."

A bit later: "This is so real..." but then he added thoughtfully: "But it's also unreal, for I live in Norway and you have your three beautiful children."

With this he sketched the difficulties he saw along the road.

Nevertheless he went for it. He has done his utmost. He is fond of the children and they are fond of him, each of them in their own way. At their first meeting it clicked between them. He calls it his mysterious bond with the children which was right there from the very beginning.

Yoram, the eldest, who's ten years old, said one morning in the shower:

"I hope Hermod wants to become my father, for I have the feeling that the two of us together can bring about some change in the world."

Hermod is exciting to him. He looks exciting, tall, wild, like a real viking. He is a medical doctor, he has travelled a lot, he has done adventurous things and he is playful like a child.

Tara, eight years old, fell in love with him immediately. She thinks he is so handsome and sweet. On her birthday he gave her a CD, to which he danced with her and swung her around.

She screamed in sheer delight: "Oh, this is what I've always wanted!"

And Imre, the little one of three and a half, wants to marry him. She often includes him in her play, then she travels to Norway on rocking horseback and brings him important letters. When she takes the phone and it is him, we can hear it through her swooningly loving voice: "Hi, Hermand, hi....!" (She always calls him Hermand)

He took care of her while I was at work. They did their shopping at the local store, where he, on her orders, carried a back pack with a huge cuddly toy dolphin. They danced together and she fell asleep on his chest.

During the last year we have seen each other about every couple of weeks, mostly for a longer period of time.

After Christmas, when we had very intense, beautiful moments together, he said that now he too wanted to go only for what is essential in life. Our relationship is part of that.

I had my tropical dream wish and my ticket in store and he

got an invitation for a conference in Jamaica, with the promising title The Conscious Universe, organised by the Scientific and Medical Network, an international organisation, of which he is a member, which promotes open exploration in science and human experience.

Although initially I would not have thought of Jamaica myself, it does have all the ingredients for the tropical dream trip. Besides, there we can do a scuba diving course as well, something which both of us have wanted for a long time. And the conference is in accordance with our interests. After some consideration - he needs a bit more time than the average person - we have decided to go. It will be a three week holiday, one week of conference, with morning sessions from 10am to 1pm, convenient for a tropical climate. And here we go.

And now we really are going, hearing the throbbing of the engines. In my reverie I have not even noticed that the plane has been standing on the ground for a long time, waiting for permission to take off. The plane starts to accelerate and leaves the ground. I close my eyes. I am flying to a new phase.

A new wind has been blowing since the decision for this trip was taken. A light, warm wind, with the sensation of a promise, that it is right between us, that it will be right. Since the New Year I have no doubts about this anymore. I found out that he had never questioned whether he wanted to be with me. There was only the question of the way we could continue to be together, for he had never been able to see a future in life.

But I have been afraid of losing him in some other way. There has been a curious fear in me since my childhood: that I would lose my partner around the age of 30. A few weeks ago Hermod called me, to say that his heart had been fibrillating for several hours. It had started after he had made himself angry at a group of young vandals. He had not been able to reach me earlier, as I had been away for the day. He had taken medicine and gone to bed. He did not want to go to hospital, he knew the medical mill that would be waiting for him there and this would not lead to any direct results.

He asked me for distant healing. After our talk my old fear came back. Do I want a relationship with someone I can lose any moment? Yes, I love him. Everyone can die. Any of us could just walk under a car. I go for this love. I let go of my fear and in doing so I set him free. Then I was able to give him healing. Shortly after our talk his heart started beating regularly again.

He told me that during these hours he had felt that he really wanted to live, something that has never been self-evident to him. He has always had difficulty in accepting the suffering on earth and the meaning or meaninglessness of existence. He has even wished himself dead. Now, he said, he felt he wanted to live. And over the phone we were, like so many times before, very close.

There is some pressure rising in my head. It is not recommended to be in a high pressure cabin with a cold. For the past weeks I have been suffering from a persistent flu, along with many other Dutch people. The wet and greyish winter weather triggered this. He phoned me every day, to ask how I was doing, my phone doctor. While I was in bed with a high fever, we had the most beautiful exchanges.

One of his very fine qualities is his curiosity, this touches upon everything. In wonder he can bend over a blade of grass and he can speak passionately on the limitations of our human nature. He can become terribly angry and desperate at the suffering in the world and he can be fiery with enthusiasm about love, beauty and a good meeting.

One morning he called to ask how I was doing. Soon it became apparent that he was the one who was depressed. He was angry at the world again and not able to get out of his bed. That night I had a dream about the suffering in the world, which moved me deeply, at the same time realising the responsibility of each of us to live our own life to the fullest, here and now and from here to contribute to the world.

Whether he was impressed by the content of my story, I do not know. But he got very excited by the idea that the two of us were so opposite in our attitude towards life, like two complementary parts, whilst working towards the same core. He said that when we combine our strengths, we may come to a marvellous creativity together.

We had reached this conclusion before. Thus he came to talk about his ideas to excite people to wonder about life, to awaken them, to provoke their curiosity by questioning what they do not know, but what they would like to know. He himself can wonder about the small miracles of life and inspire others to do the same. When someone is in the 'wonderstate', then he is open to something new, he is open to the environment and th-ere is a possibility for change and growth. In this way we can expand the borders of our consciousness. When we share our wonder, we can enter a dialogue and come to creativity together.

"... maybe one day we can give a 'wonder-workshop' together!" He sighs."... I'm so grateful that we're together, you don't know what you mean to me. Whatever I come up with, you always feel where I'm at and you're immediately on the same wavelength. Sometimes I feel like a refugee, coming staggering out of a long exile and being received and taken care of by you."

"I am just as grateful," I assured him. "You're carrying me through life with your love. I've never before felt so contained, seen and understood."

"That's mutual."

"Maybe we can write a book about our relationship one day..."

"You can write that book!"

Another morning I hardly had a voice as a result of a throat infection, but I had seen a beautiful image in my meditation the previous evening. There was silence and light. In this light emerged the image of a wet, beautiful female figure, naked in a misty space. She was sitting in a lotus of water and unfolding herself, rising slowly. The waterpetals were opening. Suddenly I realized that I was this woman (which is surprising, for usually I do not consider myself as beautiful) and I felt myself unfolding. I looked up and saw golden doors open, leading to an unknown dimension beyond. I knew I would go through these doors. There was nothing to stop me. Still the time was not yet ripe, or I was not ripe yet. In this understanding there was rest and silence.

He thought it was beautiful and said that if I could let go of my uncertainties, that I might allow myself to be beautiful, then I shall flourish.

"Now you have to rest," he said after some time. "I'll keep you in my arms until you fall asleep."

When I was free from fever, I started to pack my sarongs. It was unreal to go to the shed through the wet snow with a cold in my head and trembling knees to get my flippers. But so what, the Caribbean sun would burn away the rest of the virus.

They pass through the cabin with a snack. That is what it is called on a shorthaul flight like this. Carefully I try a bit of a small tasteless bread roll. No appetite. I confess to myself that I am a bit nervous. I am always nervous when we see each other after some weeks. I am 31 years old and in love like a teenager. Life is strange.

Yesterday evening he called around eleven o'clock, just when I wanted to go to bed. We had spoken already several times that day to discuss all kinds of practical matters. Now he called to read me a piece out of a wonderful book with dialogues on science and spirituality by Rupert Sheldrake and Matthew Fox*

'... It is about natural grace...:'

"... Meister Eckart said in the fourteenth century simply,'Nature is grace'... The universe has been a blessing and a grace for fifteen billion years... None of us had to prove our right to be here for the original

fireball to come up with the right temperature and the right rate of expansion within one millionth of a millionth of a second for us to be here. It's what the mystic Julian of Norwich said in the fifteenth century: 'We have been loved before the beginning.'...

What does grace mean? Grace is about gift. Grace is unconditional love... Grace and gratitude are really the same words. Gratia in Latin means thanks. Being grace-conscious is being grateful. Being graceful is simply living out this basic beauty of the universe. Gracefulness is a much larger category than what we usually do with the word beauty, because in our culture to be beautiful you have to be under so many pounds and you must meet all these other criteria we invent. But some of the most graceful people I've met have been very large people who are graceful in their body's movements, in their dance, in their language, and in their communication. Graceful is another word for beautiful, but it's a fuller word.

The response to grace is praise... Onye Onyemici is an African spiritual drummer who works with us in Oakland and he says: 'When you praise hold nothing back'.... Praise is very practical. Getting praise back is getting our breath back, it's about getting our energy back and it's about the capacity of letting go and rediscovering our capacity for joy and the bigness of the soul.

One more point is this: while I like to begin talking about original blessing, original grace and praise, this is not in any way to ignore suffering, evil or struggle. Just the opposite, it is all to prepare the way for dealing with it. Until we can feel graced - a psychological term for that might be high self-esteem- we're not in a position to deal with our wounds or anyone else's wounds... "

I let the meaning of the words reverberate within. The idea of natural grace is the essence of the pearl I want to find, which I know exists within, in me, in Hermod, in everyone of us.

"Thank you," I said with a sigh, "Are you also going to sleep now?" Knowing that he had postponed several odd jobs until this last day.

"No, not for a few hours. I've collected what I want to take with me, which still needs to be packed yet. I want to write a few letters, and wash the car. "

I never know when he is joking.

"Washing the car in the middle of the night?"

"Yes, I don't want to leave him like this for three weeks."

It was serious. I tried to reassure him by saying that the car probably would be cleaned by the rain, which was silly, for in Norway it does not rain in February, it only snows. And that was exactly why he wanted to take care of his car. I let it be.

"But I wish you goodnight and maybe you can give me a call in the morning to see if I'm awake. 'God natt, sov godt, og varm klem.'"

('Goodnight, sleep well and a warm hug.')

"A goodnight to you as well. At what time do you have to leave for the airport?"

"Nine o'clock at the latest."

My flight would leave a few hours later. I had the prospect of a quiet morning.

This morning, when I had just finished breakfast with the children and was about to take them to school, the phone rang.

"Hello, I'm just calling to say that I'm awake and now I'll prepare myself for leaving."

"You're early awake, how come?" I ask surprised.

"I haven't slept, ... but I've done almost everything I wanted to do."

How is it possible! We talk a few more things over.

"... see you soon in London ..."

The stewardesses pass by with the duty-free trolley. I remember that he has asked me to buy an alarm clock, which I hadn't got around to doing yet. They sell one here. A sudden hunch tells me he might have bought one on his Oslo-London flight. In itself it would not matter to have two alarm clocks, but I decide not to do it and to see whether he has bought one.

The landing has started already. The fasten seatbelt signs are on. The North Sea is just a pond isn't it? Taking off, a moment of reverie, a snack and a drink being put into your hands, landing and there we are. Slowly the aircraft empties. I take my coat and shoulder bag and set off for the luggage reclaim.

Since we are stopping over in London, we have to check in again tomorrow for the flight to Jamaica. Not particularly handy to go into London with these heavy travel bags, but he had promised he would help me carry them. The stop-over was his idea, because he wanted to visit his friends Stephen and Linda with me. Slowly I walk through the corridor to the arrival hall.

My stomach clenches for a moment. There he sits, a tall man with a wild bunch of hair, an expressive, open face and friendly blue eyes. And yes, he looks a bit tired. Who skips a night's sleep before leaving for a journey. He stands up, lightens up and opens his arms. I jump into them.

"Hi..."

For a moment the world doesn't exist.

This is how we said goodbye six weeks ago at the airport in Oslo.

"There is no time," you said then.

Now I feel it. There is no time. It is now.

London, February

Finally we let go of each other and look at each other thoroughly.

"I can hardly believe that you've been so ill, you're looking so radiant!"

"And you're looking tired."

"I'm a bit tired," he says light-heartedly.

"Sorry, I'm this late, did you have to wait for a long time?"

"No, I made some phone calls."

He always makes phone calls.

Happy and somewhat shy too we look at each other. It is so

good to see each other again. We decide to go for a drink, before we set off for Stephen and Linda.

"How was it to say goodbye to the children?"

"It was good, but difficult, as always. This morning I took Yoram and Imre to school. Yoram was very relaxed. He was looking forward to spending a few weeks with Peter. For your birthday he has made a beautiful huge drawing of Yggdrasyl, the tree of life, from the Norwegian mythology. The drawing is so big that I decided not to bring it with me right now. You'll get it when you come in April."

He laughs: "Then I'm looking forward to that!"

"Imre goes to nursery school one morning a week, you know, the one we visited one day. She doesn't realize what three weeks are, but she's strongly determined not to miss me. I was the one who found it difficult to leave her. I have a present with me, from her, for your birthday. It was all her own idea.

'One morning, a few weeks ago, she came out of her bed and said: "This is a present for Hermod's birthday, he can play with it on the beach." It's a brilliant idea, I think.'

"Did she say Hermod, not Hermand?"

"Eh, yes, Hermand of course, she still says that, we have given up trying to correct her."

"And Tara?"

"Tara isn't well, she has caught my flu, but happily she hasn't got it that badly. We spent the morning cosily together. I had to do some small jobs and afterwards I got some treats from the bakery and read her a story over a cup of tea. Then we were both so tired that we lay down on the couch, until Peter came."

"How was that?"

"Relaxed. He was looking well. He's looking forward to being with the children for a few weeks and Tara was very pleased to see him. They brought me to the station together. I left them with confidence."

"Yet it must be strange for Peter to see you leaving for a trip with me. I wonder how that feels."

"Me too." It is and remains an unnatural situation, a divorce. I wish that for nobody, certainly not for the children. However according to the circumstances, I think we're doing well all of us together, including Peter.

In the underground, on our way to Stephen and Linda, with all our luggage stuffed in between the Londoners, we huddle close together. I am aware of his energy field, it's as if I trace his field with tiny tentacles of attention, to explore him, get to know him once again. It feels so good that I have to smile.

"Are you thinking of how much I'm looking forward to seeing you in a bikini?"

I burst out laughing: "No, that's the last thing I'd think about!"

In the dark underground, between all those pale people in winter clothes, it is hard to imagine that tomorrow we shall be in the warm tropics. I still have a cold, I'm feeling tired and pale after the flu and I can't imagine myself walking along the beach in a bikini. Besides a bikini would be quite a new departure for me, having hidden myself in a swimsuit for years. And he knows this very well.

"You have brought it with you, haven't you?"

"Yes, you insisted on it, but it'll stay in my bag, I've got a beautiful new swimsuit."

"What a pity, I was so much looking forward to it."

"I was sensing your energy field, did you feel that?"

"No, but I do feel that it's very good to feel you!" and he pulls me close.

A few times he stands up to arrange our luggage in a different way, when the tube gets more and more packed with people. We have quite a lot of luggage. On top of our hand luggage I have two suitacases. That is more than I usually take with me. The second bag is only half full, there is space for his stuff. Yesterday over the phone I understood this would be necessary. I'd rather bring too little than too much, he is the opposite. He has an enormous backpack and several plastic bags with an indefinable content. Apologetically he says: "There were a few things I couldn't leave behind. And I brought a small library, I couldn't decide which books I wanted to take with me."

We laugh at it. By now we have come to know each others' habits and peculiarities. He puts some of his plastic carrier bags into my half empty travel bag and takes it over.

We change tubes a few times. I do not keep track of it, I just let myself be guided, he knows where to go. Finally we are standing at a busy, windy corner of a tube station waiting for Stephen to pick us up. It is already dark, the street lamps are on. Most of the shops are closing and people are hastily passing by. It is cold and I am shivering a little. My old black winter jacket, which I only took for the way there and back, is not too warm. He comes to stand behind me to protect me from the wind and puts his arms around me.

"You mustn't get ill again, you should wear a scarf!.

He does not speak about a warmer coat or a warmer sweater, he is a great advocate of woollen scarves.

A little later an old, shining, silver coloured Jaguar stops in front of us. A man of a moderate height, turning grey, steps out and greets Hermod with a warm embrace. We introduce ourselves. And when he opens his arms to embrace me too, I see that he has friendly, discerning brown eyes. We load our luggage and get into the car. Hermod tells him that the London underground in the rush hour looks less like a sardine tin than Stephen had made him believe. While they are talking I notice the affection between them. This will be a good evening, I know.

We drive into a quiet street, where the car stops in front of a beautiful old house in late-Victorian style. His girlfriend Linda comes to greet us with a radiant, very sweet smile. She is indeed something butterfly-like, as Hermod has depicted her. We arrive in the big room on the upper floor, with a view onto a roof terrace. We make ourselves comfortable on the couch and on the floor. And then there is this feeling of being in a familiar, yet unknown environment, with familiar, yet new friends. I know and feel that they and Hermod know each other very well.

We do not need superficialities in order to get acquainted. Within five minutes Hermod and Stephen have come to central issues of life, while I am still taking in the interior and Linda takes care of getting us something to drink. Stephen asks about my background and we get engaged in a lively dialogue on psychology and medical science.

At a certain point Hermod contributes: "In my opinion real healing takes place in a human meeting, by an attitude of unconditional love. That's what I call a good meeting, when there's an exchange from heart to heart. As a physician one can prescribe all kinds of things and help people to get rid of their symptoms, but real healing can only occur from within. That's why I try to take my time for all my patients in order to meet the human being. In my profession this is made difficult by pressure of time, we are expected to finish with the patients quickly and efficiently, but I don't want to make any concessions to this. The only commitment I want to make is the commitment to love."

While he talks I hear his passion. I know this passion in him, his longing for love, for heart-to-heart contact and his frustration that this has been made so difficult by the working conditions. His commitment to love concerns all aspects of life...

He smiles at me: "Elleke and I've been talking about this very often."

Dinner is ready by now, we go downstairs and sit down in a small cosy kitchen, where we continue our conversation while enjoying a delicious meal, prepared with care. Linda asks us curiously:

"How is it, to live in different countries?"

We exchange a knowing glance. This glance contains our whole history, including all the uncertainties, love and the growth we have been going through. He gets up to speak: "It's difficult, we phone each other a lot and try to see each other as often as possible and then for an extended period. Until now this has been okay, but we can't continue this way. There will be a moment when we'll have to take other steps..."

"Do you know which steps?"

We look at each other, this is delicate, but we know where we are standing.

"We do have ideas, but no plans yet," he says.

"When we're going to live together, the children and I will move to Norway," I add.

This became clear pretty soon. Although he is a world citizen, who has lived in several countries during his childhood and who has travelled so much in later years, he is still a real Norwegian. When we travelled through Norway last summer, hiked through the mountains, swam in the fjords, I saw that he belongs there, he is rooted there. For the children and me the rich Norwegian nature and wide space would be of great benefit. We can be replanted.

With these words they can't resist asking.

"Do you have children?"

"Yes," he answers, almost proudly, "she has three very beautiful children."

Of course I have to tell their names and how old they are.

"How did you actually meet?"

Laughingly we exchange another glance. We have different experiences of our first meeting, also of the course of events afterwards. We have had some humorous discussions about this. He gets up to speak:

"It was at a conference in Amsterdam, three years ago. I had been sitting behind her and her sister for the whole morning, without her seeing me. During the lunch break she sat at the only table were there were any empty places left. I thought this worked out well and sat down beside her. We had a long and good talk. I felt attracted to her, I thought she was a nice student.

Which she was, but she turned out to be much more. When she told me that she had a family I knew I had to be cautious. We exchanged addresses anyway. Some time later I got a card from her and I phoned her, she wrote back and I phoned again, not at all with the idea of starting a relationship, but we had beautiful exchanges and a special friendship developed. The relationship I had at that time broke down and her relationship with her - ex-husband now - grew apart. This wasn't because of me, but due to other circumstances. I came to Holland again to attend a conference and we spent some days together and gradually something developed."

"What kind of conference was that, where you met?"

"It was about dolphins and healing. Elleke and I both have an affinity with dolphins. I've swam with dolphins several times. And she has done her graduation research on the psychological effect of the interaction with wild dolphins in Australia. Last summer we had a very special meeting with a wild dolphin in Norway. We swam with him, danced with him, rode on his back and it was so loving. That really was a healing encounter."

The conversation continues amongst them.

In my thoughts I still see us with tears of emotion running over our cheeks in a slow underwater dance with this huge dolphin. The three of us were united in one consciousness, two humans and an animal. Indeed it was a transforming encounter.

What a lot we've been going through for the last year and a half. I also think of our visit to the Dalai Lama, where we attended a course last autumn. These kind of initiatives come from him, the theme of his whole life is a search for the meaning of life and for the borders of the unknown. The Dalai Lama represents to him a living example of wisdom and compassion. In that week with the Dalai Lama we discovered how much we respect each other as human beings, as man and woman, friend and partner. These were deep lessons.

The evening passes quickly. I am getting tired and notice that he - who has skipped a night's sleep - is not looking too fresh any more either. Tomorrow we have to leave for the airport on time. We agree on having breakfast together at eight o'clock. Hermod and I go up the white painted stairs to the cosy bedroom which has been prepared for us. A warm bed is waiting for us under a skylight, from our bed we can watch the sky and the clouds floating by.

"I bought an alarm clock in the plane, which we'll set up now," he says, showing me a small, handy silver coloured clock.

"I was hoping you'd done that, I didn't buy one."

He adjusts the clock and places it at the head of the bed.

As we slip in between the pink sheets, we also slip into each other's arms.

"Endelig!" "Finally!" he sighs and with his hands he gently searches the contours of my body.

"I think we should be naked."

That's what he always thinks. To me this is something symbolic, when he says this, as if we give ourselves to each other on all levels, are fully allowed to get to know each other. Tiredness melts away. Each time I am surprised how my body opens up to him like a flower to the sun.

"Now I recognise your body again," he says. "It is immediately beautiful and exciting, but now it also feels familiar again."

Once more we are everywhere inside and around each other, like on that first night.

After a tender and passionate action we silently lie together.

"Jeg elsker deg!" he sighs from the core of his heart.

"What do I hear?" I ask surprised.

Once he explained to me that in Norwegian there are two ways to say "I love you", one is more common: "Jeg er glad i deg." The other is so meaningful and intense that it isn't used that much. The latter is the one he now sighs.

"Nothing, it's a secret," he whispers and pulls me close.

With a fulfilled feeling of happiness I doze away.

This is now, I realize. This moment may last in eternity. It may stay now forever.

The next morning we are awakened by the friendly peep of our new alarm clock. We take a shower and pack our things. At eight o'clock I'm ready and go downstairs. I find Stephen in the kitchen, preparing breakfast. A hearty good morning follows.

"I'm very glad we've come to know you, I can feel your resonance. Actually we knew this in advance. Linda and I said to each other: 'When Hermod loves her, we shall too'".

"I had the same thoughts about you," I smile.

A little while later, a radiant Linda comes in. We drink a cup of tea as a start.

"Do you think our doctor will come soon, or shall we start with breakfast? This doctor is always late."

Ah, so this knowledge has arrived in Great Britain as well.

"Let's start."

When Hermod comes down a little later, we are already enjoying our croissants. "Yesterday evening you asked how we met and Hermod has told his version, well now I would like to tell mine, which is quite different...."

I look at Hermod, "... with your permission."

He nods.

"My version started before we met. I had a feeling that I would lose Peter and that I would meet another love, a big love. At that time there were no signs that Peter and I would separate, on the contrary, we had been very happy together for about 10 years and at that time we still were. Although at a later point I came to realize there had been signs that we were somewhat growing apart and we would have to give each other space.

"I went to that conference on a flash of inspiration, to see whether I could carry out my graduation research on the topic of dolphins and I was focussed on this, not on meeting someone. While I was sitting at that lunch table, all of a sudden he came walking towards me and I knew it was him. All kinds of flashes ran through my mind of a past and a future with him, it was as if I could look inside him...

"I also saw the loss of Peter, a shock, pain and sorrow, a lot of love and fulfilment. I couldn't make head or tail of it. I was very shocked and I didn't want this at all. He sat down beside me and started off talking very enthusiastically and passionately. Actually he was flirting terribly. I didn't know what was happening to me."

"Ah yes, when I'm travelling, I'm full of eros," he adds lightly.

"When he asked me whether I would like to come to Norway one day, I felt I had to tell him I had a family. Suddenly his whole attitude changed. We exchanged addresses and I sent him a card, but never heard from him and I suppressed the memory of that meeting. I took it that these flashes and images had just been my imagination. At Christmas I bought some cards for my friends abroad and while I was going through my address book I happened to find his address. He's still special, he's worth a Christmas card, I thought. One month later he called. As soon as I heard his voice, I got those flashes again, as if I was watching a film throughout time. I had the feeling I'd known him for a long time. 'I love you,' I concluded to my amazement. This feeling hasn't left me since then."

There is no time to elaborate on this any more. It is almost time to say goodbye. But Stephen and Linda understand the message behind our stories. In some way or another we have found each other and seem to belong together.

Linda will perform a dance in Stockholm next May. Hermod will probably be in Stockholm at that time as well.

"See you in May, then we'll dance together!" he says, as we walk down the stairs.

Stephen takes us to the tube station and next there is another journey with the London underground. At Gatwick Airport we check in our luggage. In the large departure hall we get acquainted with a group of British people from the Scientific and Medical Network, who are also going to the conference. Hermod knows some of them from previous conferences and meetings. We buy some stationary so as to be able to take notes during the conference. Finally - it has become something of a tradition - we have to run to the gate. This time, too, it turns out the plane is delayed, for an unknown time. Arriving at the gate we find a place to sit quietly in between many waiting people.

I decide now is the time to give him Imre's present for his birthday. I hand him a small parcel in crinkled paper and emphasize again that this is her own spontaneous idea. He opens it carefully. It is a small blue seahorse, for making sandcastles. Just right for this holiday.

He kisses it: "Thank you, Imre! I love seahorses so much!"

Being together time flies and after a while we are allowed to board. The atmosphere is already somewhat Caribbean. The cushions and plates on the chairs are in bright, tropical colours, Caribbean music sounds from the speakers and many Jamaicans colourfully dressed are coming on board. As pleased as Punch we sit down. This is the first time we fly together. Usually we fly to each other. We have spoken about flying together in a symbolic way, to be free together. On this journey we'll fly together and dive together, high and deep, the whole spectrum. It will be good.

The plane is made ready for take off and we fasten our seatbelts. When I look out of the window everything outside looks grey and gloomy. Bye, bye, wet, wintery London!

Once in the air we get a drink and a meal. We talk, and study the book that will be the theme of the conference. I read, he watches films, we listen to music and are very content with all this. Gradually sleep overcomes us. I fold my legs in my chair. He is tall, now he can sit diagonally and use the space in front of my chair for his legs. I lie with my head and chest on his lap and in his arms, curled up and cherished like a baby. A blanket covers us and together we doze off. Time flies.

Much faster than the hours on our watches indicat,e we have crossed the Atlantic and landing in Jamaica has started.

Here evening has just fallen and it is dark outside. Through the window I see the black ocean and where the island begins a messy pattern of the lights of Kingston. The aircraft comes to a stop on the runway and we walk to the arrival hall. Warmth is rising from the asphalt. The warm, velvet-like tropical evening air strokes our faces and penetrates our clothes. The tights feel suddenly unnatural on my legs. Despite the fact that we have come to a town I smell sweet, tropical scents of humid earth and vegetation. It smells unfamiliar and promising. I get a shiver of excitement.

"We're here," I whisper.

He puts his arm around me and kisses me on the top of the head:

"Welcome to Jamaica!"

The arrival hall is big, wide and messy. Black people are walking all over the place with bouncing steps, quite a difference from the more stiff, pale Europeans. We join the group of British people that has gathered outside on the car park to depart together by minibus to Frenchman's Cove, the place where the conference will be held. Soon we drive over a bumpy, winding mainroad through the dark night. The windows of the bus are open, the sultry wind of the night is blowing in my face. Between the bushes now and then I see a bit of black sea glittering in the dark and here and there a house.

We sit close behind the driver and get acquainted with the people sitting behind us. Hermod is talking to David, the director of the conference and of the Network about new ways of learning and development, curiosity and wonder. They have known each other for some time and obviously there is a warm mutual affection between them. I let my thoughts wander.

My curiosity and wonder concern the here and now. I am

trying to grasp the fact that I am here.

Gradually tiredness attacks. It is around midnight here, but our biological clocks are indicating that we are moving towards next morning. Little by little the conversations die down. Half asleep I feel him sinking against me and lying his head on my lap. I put my arm around him.

Continuously Afro-American songs are sounding from the speakers in the front of the bus. Ordinary life seems far away and unrealistic, we slide into a timeless dream, in which there is nothing but a bumpy road winding through an unfathomable darkness.

Suddenly the bus makes a sharp turn and stops in front of the entrance of an estate. We are there!

Waiting for the group to finish checking in, I sit down on a wall outside the reception under an enormous tree, which has a number of lianes are hanging down. Behind the crowns of the trees I see a clear sky and twinkling stars. They seem brighter and closer than I am used to. Now I can hear the sounds of the tropical night, crickets and tree frogs, and the rippling sound of a stream I cannot see. The air is still warm and sultry.

It is fascinating to arrive at night at a new place and not be able to see where one is, but to be dependent on other senses.

Then we are shown to our appartment, which turns out to be a huge bungalow in a secluded part of the estate. In amazement we stick the key in the lock and go inside. Beforehand Hermod had carefully let David know that he would be coming with his girlfriend and that we would appreciate some privacy. David has been generous. This house is beyond all expectations. We enter a living room as wide as a ballroom, with a shining, polished floor of natural stone tiles, walls and stylish rattan furniture. Windows from ceiling to the ground offer an ocean view. Via two stone steps we come into a large bedroom with a kingsized bed. The wall opposite the bed is made of sliding glass doors, leading out to a balcony.

We open the doors and look straight over the ocean. A mild, salty smell greets us. The moon casts a silvery shine on the water.

In front of us, on the edge of the cliffs a palm tree's black silhouette stands out against the dark blue sky. We hear the waves crashing against the rocks below. The only sounds are the wind and the ocean.

I walk to the balustrade and he comes and stands behind me and puts his arms around me. I lean my head against his breast.

Silently and almost respectfully we take everything in.

After having stood like this for some time I break the silence:

"We've arrived in paradise."

"Yes, it's incredible! Every time I'm astonished how circumstances work out when we are together."

"I think this is your influence, it's you who got the invitation for this conference, you're the one who spoke to David. You always get everything done. Thank you for bringing me here."

"I thank you for stimulating me to go on a trip."

"Maybe that's the right dynamics between us, I incite you to action and you decide what to do and where to go."

We go inside again and close the doorway with a sliding screen of wire gauze. We leave the curtains open, the view of the ocean is too enchanting to hide behind curtains. With a fresh shower we wash off the sweat and tiredness of the journey. It has turned deep into the night by now.

Naked we slip in between the clean sheets.

Jamaica, Frenchmen's Cove, February.

We wake up in bright daylight. From our bed we can see the turquoise ocean, smooth as a mirror and we hear the sound of the waves crashing on the cliffs. The sky is sheer blue and the sun is shining. It is too inviting to stay in bed for long. We take a shower and rummage about in our luggage in search of light clothes as we tidy away our clothes and clutter into the cupboards. I hang my two colourful sarongs over the chairs, as a personal touch to the house.

"I forgot our alarm clock!" he exclaims.

That is a pity. In my memory I see it standing at the head of the bed at Stephen and Linda's. I even thought, we should not forget about it, but we did.

As soon as we are dressed, we explore our house in more detail. Behind the house we discover a second terrace, in the midst of lush vegetation, big yellow flowers, ferns and lianes, overlooking a beautiful small bay with a white sandy beach and a view of the ocean on the other side. We name this terrace our 'jungle terrace' and for some moments we stand in wonder.

It is nearly ten o'clock. Breakfast is served until ten in the main house, where the conference will be held . We step into our leather slippers and walk down the path, which winds down along the side of the bay. We pass the bay and at the other side we follow the path up to where the main house lies on a hill.

On a terrace under a wide roof there are several tables, where some people are still having breakfast. There is a table with tea and coffee, toast, butter, cheese, slices of cake and a rich selection of fruits; bananas, pineapple, papaya, grapefruit, and melon. While we enjoy the delicious fruits and the view of the luxuriant plant growth, some graceful black birds with bright yellow beaks and elegant tails come to sit on the balustrade and sing to us.

After breakfast we decide to take a short exploratory trip round the estate. We follow the coastline of the high cliffs, watching the ocean. Everything is new and different, the trees with their big green leaves and lianes, the birds, the butterflies, the insects. Here and there I recognise a plant which we tend to keep in our homes in Europe, but these are giants in comparison with the plants at home. No wonder, in this sunny, humid climate, everything grows in abundance. I feel pity for our house-plants, which have to grow in between four walls in a pot.

Our senses are wide open to all new impressions as well as to each other. We drink each other. Although we have only been together for two days now, it feels as if we have never been without each other.

Slowly we walk back to the bay. The turquoise water looks tempting and the sun starts to burn our skin. We decide to spend the rest of the day quietly on the beach and go back home to get our swimming gear. There are some people on the beach, but it is not crowded. The beach is like the scenery in a film, a small, secluded bay, with fine white sand, a palm tree here and there.

On one side of the bay a river flows out into the sea, here the water is brackish and shallow. There is another tiny little sandy beach on the other side of the river, surrounded by high trees and lianes. Singing birds are flying low over the water. We spread out our towels and run into the water. Even the water has a pleasant temperature and is crystal clear. We swim out of the bay. The sea is smooth like a mirror. The sandy bottom is white with some seaweed covered rocks here and there. There are no sharks or dangerous fish in this area. We snorkel and tumble around. Once back into shallow water, where he is able to stand, we put our arms around each other and dance and dash around in a long embrace. Back on the beach we rub ourselves with suncream and stretch out on the towels.

"It's a beautiful swimsuit, but I feel sorry for this poor little belly, which is not allowed to be in the sun."

"We have talked about this before. Let me be. I feel more comfortable in a swimsuit."

"Still it's a pity!"

We lie down. Let us simmer in the sun and life is fine. The salt tingles on my skin. Nothing is better for a lasting winter flu than salt water and warm sunshine, I decide. And nothing is better for jet-lag than a relaxed day on the beach.

A little later: "Now it's time to play with Imre's seahorse. I'll practise and you have to take pictures, so that she can see how I'm progressing."

He takes out the blue seahorse and seriously starts to fill it with moist sand. It has a small detailed shape and the seahorses come out somewhat crumpled. Gradually a row of small heaps of sand comes into being, which begin to look more and more like seahorses. Then it is my turn. As a mother I am a bit more experienced in making sandcastles, I think personally. I also make a few. It is fun!

Memories of Dutch beach days with the children are bubbling up. I see some Jamaican children are splashing with their parents in the water.

"The children would have found it fantastic here."

"Yes, this is a marvellous place for children, safe and secluded."

"I miss them a little, when I see those families here. On the other hand it is also a privilege, and right now a necessity, to have time for the two of us. But you know, we'll probably always have this privilege, the children will sometimes be with Peter in the future."

He sighs: "I think it's complicated all those relationships. I'm not just going for one relationship, but for five. In a way it's also a relationship with Peter. I feel a lot of sympathy for him, but I absolutely don't know how to relate to him."

"Accept him as the father of the children. There's no problem for them. They've already given both of you a place. He's their father and you are... more a friend and a little bit of a father figure as well."

"Yes, that's what I would like to be, a friend, someone who takes care of them and who takes responsibility ... and a little bit of a father as well... What I find difficult is how I can give shape to my humble authority. You have all your rules and patterns already, which you have grown together."

"In my perception you have the same authority as I do," I reassure him. "We can make the agreement always to stay in line with each other and not to desert each other in the presence of the children. If there is a difference in opinion we can discuss it afterwards and decide which line to stick to in the future."

"Hmm, that's right, but in some ways I'm still so immature myself."

"Maybe you can grow up in this together with the children."

He nods thoughtfully.

Early afternoon a Caribbean lunch is served in tents on the beach. We eat some rice, fish, marinated vegetables and salad. The topic of the children is still on our minds. While having lunch he talks about a nice day he spent with one of his nephews, his brother's three children , and he emphasises the importance of spending time with each child individually.

"That's another problem: you have so many children that it will be difficult for me to take each of them for a day out and then also have time with my nephews!"

This makes me laugh:

"We can divide the tasks and make combinations of children of the same age, you can take one or two of them out and I'll spend a nice time with the rest, or the other way round."

He can also see some fun in this.

When we have finished our meal we return to our beach towels.

"Then we may have our own little one too. When we have a child together I would want to work less, maybe half time, so that I can be with the baby as much as possible..."

The way he says this touches me. We have talked about having a child together before. At the very beginning of our relationship he asked me whether I could imagine having any more children. Together with him, yes, I could imagine it. What he says now sounds well thought through. I haven't heard him say that he would want to work less, before.

"... wouldn't the other children be jealous then, because I would spend more time with the baby than with them?"

Before I can answer, he answers himself:

"Maybe they'll think it natural, because babies do need more care."

"I think so too. Besides during the day they are at school and they come back late afternoon."

He looks relieved. I nestle myself in his armpit.

"With three children you have caught up with your brother in one move."

"Yes, I've thought of that too."

"It seems a good idea to speak out our thoughts and fears to each other around this. It won't always be easy, but when we share it, we'll get through this. Don't you think?"

"Yes."

We bathe in the sun and the sea and play with the frisbee. Late in the afternoon we go back home. We only have to walk up the path to the entrance of the bay. I skip along the path, stretching my arms out to the sun. "Are you sure you want to live in Norway? You love the sun so much!"

"Yes, I'm sure... it's your country and I love it. The beauty and the space compensates for the cold. And we can go to visit the sun in winter, can't we!"

"That's true. We do this in Norway, to be able to stand the long winters."

We wash off the salt under the shower and take a warm bath together afterwards. A little later we sit on the balcony with a glass of fruit juice and some chocolate.

" It's worth the effort of travelling here even for one day," he sighs with contentment.

"Yes, one day like today and all flu and tiredness of the last weeks have disappeared."

"Why can't we always live like this? That should be possible, shouldn't it?"

"It should be, we only have to learn how."

Silently the evening falls. We go to bed early.

He lies behind me with his arms around me.

"Yesterday, when I spoke with David, he referred to you as my fiancée. I told him that you're still my girlfriend. Then we looked at each other a bit shy and laughed, ... because we don't know yet whether you'll become my fiancée... "

I lie silently, not knowing what to say. At the very beginning of our relationship he said already that - despite his fear of commitment - for the first time of his life he felt he had a relationship which made him longing for marriage and children. And he indicated, or rather stated, that when we think of having a child together, he wants to get married first. He is thinking about it now, I realize.

"This touches me," I say finally, "Inside I already chose you a long time ago. But I haven't thought of the concept of fiancée yet. The first time I got married I was so young, it was more a formality to me, while the love I felt was real, it is still there. But since I've been with you the concept of marriage has got a much deeper dimension."

We do not say anything more. In the way he holds me closer to him I feel his seriousness and tenderness.

Early in the morning we are freshly awakened by the daylight. From our bed we watch the wide ocean. We decide to go for a swim first, and at this early time of the day we have the whole bay for ourselves. After a shower I do some yoga on the jungle terrace. Since my teenage years I have meditated and practised yoga. It is as natural to me as breathing. He wants to join me. That is unique. Quietly we do some postures together. Afterwards we set ourselves down for a meditation, which we have done more often together. In silence we go our way, opening ourselves to the space within and around us. On the small terrace high on the cliffs, in between the lush green we are in our concentration a part of the environment.

It is Saturday and we have another day off ahead of us, before the conference starts. We decide to spend the morning quietly at the beach, to go to the nearby town, Port Antonio, in the afternoon and to join the group for a reggae evening. Tired and content we come home late at night.

"That was a surprising discovery, we can dance together!" I say, still relishing the memory.

"It was wonderful! And you were looking very beautiful and attractive. That black dress of yours suits you very well and fits every occasion!"

We walk the path along the bay in the direction of our house. The moonlight gives a silvery shine to the water. I cannot resist the view, I run to the beach and in one move I pull off my dress and underwear.

The water is still pleasantly warm and fluorescent where I move my hands and feet. I feel like a sea-nymph, surrounded by a light green veil. He gets into the water too. We continue our dance, slowly, in our own rhythm, carried by the water. There is no wind, only the sound of the waves. The beach looks silver, the black silhouette of a palm tree stands out against the nightblue sky. Only the moon is witness to our love.

"It is hardly comprehensible, to be as happy I feel," I whisper.

"We are in paradise," he whispers back. "On earth I can't imagine being closer to paradise than this, here, with you."

2

The Pearl

Moving between
the shores
of our hearts
the ocean
of love

In the deep
the pearl
Potential
of two souls
merging together
Potential
of each soul
individually
as a whole

It is Sunday morning and the conference starts today. It is led by Dean Radin, author of 'The Conscious Universe', a comprehensive survey of scientific research into the paranormal.* The morning is spent on an overview of the history of research on 'psi': extrasensory perception phenomena. These phenomena are as old as mankind. Serious research on this has been done for more than a hundred years now, providing evidence that these kind of phenomena do exist, but since this does not fit within our conventional paradigm, science closes her eyes.

Each morning is fascinating. A lot of information is given on experiments with different types of 'psi' phenomena. Personally this intrigues us less, instead we are intrigued by the limitations of our human understanding. It seems to be possible to obtain information without using our regular senses, by telepathy or clairvoyance. It raises the possibility that mind can transcend the limits of time and space and influence matter. It seems that a meaningful relationship exists between 'psi' abilities, intuition and creativity.

These 'psi' abilities could change our whole society, but a radical shift in world view will be necessary to accommodate this evidence. For example in psychology and medical science, it is possible that conscious intention and also unconscious emotions and thoughts can affect human health. Dean presented some remarkable evidence that mental healing can work at a distance both in space and time. This may have huge consequences for medical science.

Our minds, individually and collectively, seem to be involved in creating the world around us. The universe is like an organism of which every particle is potentially conscious of the whole and underlying everything is a profound interconnectedness. In his book Dean concludes:

Underlying the isolated world of ordinary objects and human experience is another reality, an interconnected world of intermingling relationships and possibilities. This underlying reality is more fundamental – in the sense of being the ground state from which everything originates – than the transient forms and dynamic relationships of familiar experience.

Each morning we are absorbed by these challenging ideas. The afternoons we spend near the sea or we go on a trip to explore the environment and the culture.

One afternoon there is a discussion on the beach about the social, economic and environmental problems of Jamaica. We are uncomfortably aware that we are privileged tourists in a poor and troubled country. We hold meditations on the welfare of Jamaica and by going out and spending money we support the local establishments, but our contribution is all too meagre.

One evening we take a walk to a hotel-restaurant on a hill. A small winding path indicates the way. In the moonlight we are just able to distinguish the holes and bumps. On either side of the path are thick bushes. On top of the hill there would be a wonderful view, we have been told but we do not see anything of this in the dark. Mainly we hear sounds of crickets and we smell scents of jasmine and bananas. I enjoy the stroll, but I cannot withdraw from being aware of his tension. There is a dark cloud hanging around his head, which is visible and tangible even in the dark. When I stumble against him, he reacts in an irritated way.

"What's the matter with you?" I ask.

"It's all so beautiful, peaceful and paradisical. It's almost too beautiful. There's nothing to be afraid of, nothing to be angry about. Every feeling of negativity can only come from within myself, I can't blame anything else for it and that's confronting. Now and then I just close off."

He picks a big yellow flower and sticks it in my hair.

"In itself it's not so amazing, you've had these moods for your whole life, one can't expect this to change all of a sudden. It takes time to open up to life."

"I'm getting so tired of it. Even here I can't just be happy. I'm resisting any change. I don't really believe that I am able to change. And I do not really see how it can continue between us, either. Maybe it is too ideal to try to stay in the present and see how things develop. There's nothing in life which attracts me!"

In the meantime we have arrived at the restaurant and find a table outside on the terrace, with a view of the dark hills. We order a meal.

I sigh and think back to the many talks we have had when he has been in depressive mood. Usually when he felt depressive he withdrew from the world, sometimes for days, but he did phone me. We could be duelling with words for hours about the meaning of life in which I would plead for life and he against it. Once I got tired after one and a half hours of tough discussion. I asked:

"Can you say something sweet now as a closure?"

"Hmmm, yes... maybe this: the sweetness in your heart is so big, that I can let my sourness come out and come in touch with my own sweetness. I'm so grateful to you, I only hope that the sweetness in my heart is big enough to let you have your sourness coming out as well."

With this answer I could get through the day.

Six months ago we once had a real argument: He could not find life worth living, because there is too much suffering on earth. I concluded that, in that case, he did not find our relationship worthwhile either. But according to him this did not correlate. He thought our relationship was worthwhile, but not life. I did not understand how he could separate these two. But he sometimes talked about continuing our relationship in another reality. A fascinating idea, but we are living here now.

These kind of discussions were tiring, but valuable. We always came out of it better than we started, with new inspiration and insights. This gave both of us trust. The last few months had been better. During our talks at Christmas about love being the essence of life, the decision to go to Jamaica together, the hours when his heart was fibrillating... he had come to a decision, the decision to live ... to live together.

The flower has slipped out of my hair. I put it in the middle of the table and sigh once more.

"I thought we'd left this behind us now that finally you had chosen to live and chosen our relationship."

"Yes, but right now I just don't feel this. I'm just throwing out what I feel."

He sits like a granite rock. We duel a bit further, but at a certain moment I am done with it. I do not want to hear again that there is nothing in life which attracts him, after all our beautiful moments and love tokens.

"Sometimes it seems as if we are going around in circles!" I say, somewhat irritated too.

"Well, I don't agree with that. To me these are spirals and every time we come a step forwards. I really appreciate the patience you show with me during these discussions."

"Oh?... " I'm surprised at this sudden turnaround. "Okay, if this is still the case, then I'm still willing to go through these struggles together."

We pay and walk back in a lighter mood. He puts his arm around me. I should not let him get a rise out of me, I realize. Each time we will get through it. Everyone has his own peculiarities.

It is dangerous along the road in the dark. People drive like crazy. He is more alert and careful than I am and frequently he pulls me back to the side.

I go for a swim. The moon is full now. He is sitting on the beach and watches quietly. The whole environment is breathing out peace. True peace, can only come from within, I contemplate, and nature invites us to it.

In the beginning of the second week he feels irritated for a couple of days, he critises everything I do and withdraws into himself. I take it personally and want to talk about it. Irritation makes me uncertain. There is a little girl inside.

"Although it is paradise here, it doesn't mean that I always feel paradisical and we don't always have to talk about this! That can also dissolve by itself. We can't always be in tune. I just want some more space and to spend some more time with the others."

"That's fine with me. I like to have some space for myself too. But just tell me then, take some space, don't snarl at me for nothing... I can't stand that very well."

That afternoon, just before lunch, I go and pay for our stay and show him the bill. He gets angry, he had wanted to finish off the payment himself and check the bill beforehand instead of afterwards.

I feel sad and offended. When we order our lunch at the tent on the beach, the waiter asks where we want to sit. I point towards a table apart from the others:

"Over there maybe..."

The waiter starts setting the table. Hermod sees it and bursts out: "Don't think that I want to talk with you about anything. I'm going to sit with the others!"

He stands there like a god of thunder out of the Norwegian pantheon.

Tears fill my eyes.

"We don't have to talk, but I need to get my breath back first and I'm not able to converse nicely with other people right now. What's happening? There's no reason to have these outburst sagainst me all the time."

"So I have to sit with you, because you can't stand my anger?"

I do not know what to say so I go and sit at the empty table to eat. He comes to sit at the table too, but does not touch his food.

His face is unyielding and his eyesare like steel.

"It seems as if we're testing each other's strength!"

"Well, it doesn't feel like that to me, I haven't felt so vulnerable and uncertain with you before."

"Now I feel caught in a trap, for I'm a shit if I leave you alone now."

"You're not a shit. I just can't cope very well with you when you're behaving so aggressively."

I eat my food without tasting it. As soon as I am finished he leaves with his plate to join the others' table. I go back to our villa to fetch my swimming gear and lie down on the beach in my bikini. I have not dared to wear it yet, but I cannot feel more vulnerable than I do now, so what. The jerk!

I stand up and go for a long swim. In the water my anger cools off. In fact there is nothing serious. Okay, he has been irritated and unreasonable for the last few days. Is that so terrible? It is very human. And I know I cannot stand it very well when people are angry with me. It was like this when I was a child and it has never disappeared completely.

Hermod has his moods and I know he needs space. Giving people space is not my strongest side, but I do want to learn it. I need space for myself too. Actually I cannot stand any disharmony. Everything always has to be happiness and peace. I always want to have contact, open and friendly contact. Inside there is a tiny girl who wants to be loved and liked all the time. No, little Elleke, with this man you will have to stay firmly on your feet. I love him, I feel it clearly.

Back on the beach I stealthily look in his direction. He is still busy talking. I doze off in the warm sun.

"Hi..."

I wake up with a shock. There he stands, shyly, in his arms a borrowed beachball and his frisbee.

I suppress a smile.

"Oh, hello..."

"How are you?"

"Much better. How are you?"

"Also much better. I feel so silly," he sighs.

"Me too."

"Will you come and play?"

Now I cannot suppress my laughter.

"Yes!"

Somewhat ill at ease we start playing beach ball. Soon we smack out all bits of remaining tension and become more and more jolly. Then we play with the frisbee for a long time and afterwards we decide to go for a swim.

I go into the water first and wait there for him. When I look behind, I see him swimming past me, without looking at me and with a stern face. I feel uncertain again. Is he still angry? He swims towards the open sea where the water is very rough and disappears out of sight. I become concerned and swim after him.

At the end of the bay I climb on to a rock. Far away I see a head disappearing behind the waves. A man in a boat passes by screaming that I should go back into the bay for the water is too wild today. I point to Hermod. The man sails to him. Much later he returns. We meet at the beach.

"What was the matter?" I ask concerned.

He looks as concerned as I do:

"I thought you'd angrily swum out of the bay, I was worried and went to look for you, because the water is pretty wild."

"I was waiting for you here, but thought that you were still angry and pretended not to see me, when you swam by."

We look at each other. This was very silly and unnecessary.

"I love you and I'm not at all angry any more. I thought it very sweet when you came to ask me to come and play."

"I love you ... I thought it sporty that you were willing to play at once. And this bikini suits you very well."

We do not talk much any more that day. There is nothing that needs to be said. We enjoy being together and give each other more space then before. It does not go without saying any more that we sit next to each other, or have breakfast at the same table. We get to know some more people a little better and there are nice conversations. He shows more consideration for me and does not act out so much any more. I realize both of us have learned a basic lesson.

In the sea we dance in each other's arms. Connectedness.

"Don't you feel we just belong together!?" I sigh.

He stares earnestly and intensely.

"Hmm, yes. .... But something inside of me is afraid to lose myself and to surrender completely."

"In love one can't lose oneself, one can only win oneself."

A bit later when we come out of the water, I have thought it through.

"There's a difference between giving oneself out of emotional dependency or out of unconditional love. In the first way one can lose oneself and one doesn't do justice to the other person either. In the second way there is a mutual sharing and growth into wholeness. Sometimes we do the first, but there's also the other quality of giving and we're growing towards this more and more."

A bit later I find in a book I brought with me by Eva Pierrakos*, a piece on emotional rigidity, indifference and sometimes aggression, which may develop as a defence against pain. This can prevent one from enjoying beauty and giving and receiving love. One is not able to feel the spark and rejects, when one feels safe and accepted, in order to feel the martyrdom of being rejected. The pain of being rejected is known and easier to bear than the intensity of love and being happy. It is so recognisable. I read it out to him. He says this is a game he has always played in relationships involuntarily withdrawing and rejecting when he felt safe. In this way he has never surrendered to love.

"Let's play another game," I propose, "discovering new dimensions in love."

He smiles.

In the afternoon we come to sit next to John, director of a Department of Cognitive Science in London. Amongst other things he carries out research on neurofeedback and psychoneuroimmunology and hypnosis. Hermod and I are very interested in his work and we get engaged in an animated talk. I tell him about my work with meditation and the paper I wrote for my graduation on the physiological effects of altered states of consciousness.

When lunch is over we have not finished talking yet and decide to continue our talk over the next days. Later in the afternoon I see John sitting on his own near the water and approach him. Our talk causes some ideas to bubble up in my mind and I ask him whether he knows what kind of research in this field is being done in Holland. Possibly I would be interested in participating. Enthusiastically we exchange ideas. He asks whether I would come over to London, if he offered me a job.

"Maybe.... " I respond.

Briefly I sketch my family situation and explain that Hermod and I are not living together yet, but are thinking about it now. Can he possibly use a physician with experience in hypnotherapy too? He was already charmed by Hermod and now he gets really enthusiastic. There are different projects coming up, starting next September, in which Hermod as well as I could participate. We agree to think it over.

At home I find Hermod and ask him casually whether he would be interested in doing research together in London if John could offer us a job.

"Maybe... ," he says thoughtfully, "is this the case?"

I sketch the talk on the beach. It is quite overwhelming for both of us. We decide to let it digest a bit and elaborate it further with John tomorrow.

At night I lie awake for a long time thinking about the research job. The next morning we continue talking about it. He begins to see more and more possibilities around it. Besides Stephen and Linda, he has more friends in London and in the past he has had plans to live there and work with them. He knows an area in London where it is nice to live, that would also be nice for the children. Probably it will not be that difficult to find a house there.

We are standing in the bathroom brushing our teeth and I look at him searchingly in the big mirror. In our enthusiasm about the work we have not discussed the implication of the step to live together. Or is this avoidance behaviour? The nonchalant way in which he mentions the children now makes me curious.

"Aren't you afraid of living together so soon?"

For a moment it is silent.

"No," he says in a slow, definite and teasing tone, "At first I was, yesterday, when you started talking about it, but not any more. On the contrary, I think it's a very good opportunity to start together on neutral ground, in between our countries. After a year we can always see whether we stay in London or go back to Norway. This could be a good first step."

My mouth falls open in amazement, how simple it can be! To counterbalance I tell him of my doubts, I do not want to work full time, I also want to be there for the children and maybe to enroll in some other activities. That is what I call play time.

"I can take care of the children too, we can share some of the care. I'd like to have some time as well, to be able to do other things besides the job."

At the meeting we agree with John to elaborate on it further with the three of us the next morning at breakfast. This is the last day of the conference. John is leaving for England tomorrow.

It is Saturday, there is another reggae evening at Dragon Bay nearby. We walk there in the afternoon to swim and snorkel. After a while my knee starts to ache. Like a true hero and concerned doctor he carries me on his back the rest of the swimming trip through the bay. When we arrive at the beach I ask him what I owe him for this pleasant transport.

"Three hugs and a kiss... at a moment I indicate."

Dusk is falling. We dress for the evening and enjoy a tropical cocktail. After the swim he has his attractive wet-look again. I tell him.

"And you are a Dutch version of a tropical beauty."

Time for the first hug.

"For how long have we actually been together?" he asks gently.

"Well, that depends whether you count from the first time we met, three years ago, or from our first days together, or... "

"No, I mean, including all our past lives!"

"Oh, ... I remember at least three, ... so, eh, a few hundred maybe?"

"Hmm, let's add another couple of hundred!" he says, now earnest.

We look at each other for a moment in timelesness.

"Yes," I reply simply.

Dinner has finished and live music starts. We do not hesitate, we kick off our shoes and start dancing. There are some people dancing at the side of the stage, under the palmtrees, but I pull him into the middle, in the spotlights.

"You're not shy at all!" he exclaims surprisedly.

"No, I learned that from you... and from this country, everything here is so natural, lush and extravagant. I feel free."

We dance and let go of ourselves entirely. Our bodies and movements smoothly adjust to each other. We dance until we have no breath left any more. Sweat is streaming down his face. He looks radiant like I have never seen him before.

It is almost time to go back.

"Shall we go for a little walk?"

We walk along the water line and a little further we find a rock to sit on.

"Now I want the second hug and a kiss," he demands.

It turns out to be a very tender kiss and a long embrace.

"Ik houd van je, ("I love you")" I say in Dutch.

"I love you too."

At home in bed it is time for the third hug, in which we fully merge together. I feel his love and his strength.

Still quivering from happiness, I whisper in Dutch:

"Wat ben je toch een prachtig mooi wezen..." But I realize that this is probably too difficult for him to understand and decide to repeat it in English:

"What a beautiful, wonderful being you are..."

Though he is already half a sleep. Very sleepy it sounds:

"Doei, ... doei, doei...." ("Bye, ..., bye, bye...." in pure Dutch dialect.)

A bit later he has one more revival, he turns around and gives me a final resounding kiss:

"Good night again, en slaap lekker!" ("... and sleep well!")

When I wake up the next morning, he is not lying beside me. I find him lying on his back on the jungle terrace, staring at the tops of the trees.

"Today I'll lead our meditation. We'll start in a quarter of an hour. You may do some yoga on your own first, or go swimming, but after fifteen minutes you have to be back."

A quarter of an hour later we are sitting on chairs with our backs facing each other. It will be a guided meditation of about one hour. I am curious.

"First we focus our attention on our senses, the images of the surroundings, the sounds, the scents, the taste in our mouth, the contact of the skin with our clothes and with the chair and the floor...

Then we focus the attention inwards, on the silence within...

Silence.

We imagine on one side, our dark side, all our pain, fear, anger, and sadness of our past, our present and our future. We observe it and allow it to be, without any judgement..."

Silence.

"Then we turn to our other side, our light side and imagine all our joy, hope, trust and loving experiences of our past, present and future. We observe it and allow it to be, without judgement..."

Silence.

"We turn to the middle and let both sides expand, until they touch and merge into each other. They contain our whole personal reality. Then we let this reality of dualistic feelings shrink and become as little as a tiny dot. We contain it and transcend it, experiencing Being...."

Silence.

"Now we focus our attention on our heart and each other's heart and feel the connection of love between us. We allow the energy between our hearts to circulate, nurturing and inspiring, and we let it spiral outwards, wider and wider flowing out into the universe..."

A long silence.

"We bring our attention back to our breathing and feel the

gravity which keeps our bodies down to earth. We feel our feet on the floor..."

For a long time we sit in silence. Then we get up and embrace. A long time, a timeless time.

I am deeply impressed. Not only has it been a powerful experience, I felt his heart, his whole being, during the exercise. I felt him inside, just as I feel myself and felt that he was experiencing the same with me. We were containing each other, receiving each other.

We have had these kinds of intimate experiences often before. However never before has our love been so tangible. There seems to be a force emerging, which is radiating out into the environment. We are not only together for each other, but for a larger purpose as well. This is the potential between us, which both of us have felt from the beginning. This meditation reveals his inner processes, which impress me too. I still feel him inside. It is as if we do not have to talk any more, words are no longer necessary.

"Thank you... it was, it is very beautiful. I don't know what more to say about it."

"I thank you too."

After a swim we step out of the water and joyfully I let the water splash with my feet, so the drips twinkle in the sun rays. He stops me:

"Ssshhhh, just stand still.... We are behaving as if it's normal that we are here now, stepping out of the water, like we do every day, but it is not. It is very special that we are here. We are here NOW. This is timeless."

It is time to go for breakfast. We find John at the table and join him. He tells us, especially Hermod, in more detail what it is about. He suggests that there is also a possibility for one of us, Hermod for example, to start first and for me to join in a later project, when we are a bit more settled. This appeals to me. In this way I can first concentrate on helping the children adjust to their new environment.

Within one and a half weeks John will know whether the first project, which will start in September, will go ahead. He will call us as soon as we are back. We say goodbye.

The last evening with the group we go out for dinner. In front of the terrace there is a huge flowering tree where a colony of hummingbirds is feeding in the dusk. Like blue butterfies they flutter around the big red flowers. The whole tree is covered with blue wings. The moon rises low in the pale blue sky. Hermod comes to stand behind me and whispers in my ear:

"Just for this tree it's worth coming here."

It becomes silent on the terrace.

I realize what these two weeks have done to me. The pearl has been found, my pearl and the pearl in our love. An inner peace has set in and I feel more free than ever before.

A lot of old insecurities have fallen away. Of course this is not only due to these two weeks, there have been years preceding. It is as if this experience of love and beauty, rest and space and the many meditations have completed the process. Where to go from here? There are several wonderful openings. Briefly I share my reflections with him.

Today is the day to say goodbye to Frenchmen's Cove. After breakfast we pack our things and heartily say goodbye to the others. We have become like one big family. See you at the next meeting of the Network.

I have decided to become a member as well.

Hermod has managed to arrange transport to our next destination, Negril. A driver arrives with a car to take us to Montego Bay. We load our luggage and leave Frenchmen's Cove with pain in our hearts. I realize I would not have minded staying another week. But we want to see some more of the country and take a scuba diving course in Negril. Life goes on.

The landscape passes quickly. We follow the coastal road and pass several smallvillages with here and there a house, stalls with bananas, coconuts and conch shells. Palm trees, plantations and hills are flowing by.

During the trip we hardly talk. The driver is not a talkative type of person. We see that he is tired and do not want to distract him too much from driving. We watch the landscape unfolding before our eyes. I get nauseated by the abrupt accelerations and the sudden slamming on the brakes at every hole or bump in the road. I lie down with my head in his lap and he puts his arm around me. Cherished I fall asleep.

Towards the evening we arrive at Montego Bay, where another driver waits for us. Hermod calls the guest house once more, to check if the reservation has come through correctly. When he comes back, he says:

"It's good that I phoned, they hadn't even understood we are a couple."

This new driver is fresh, cheerful and curious:

"A couple, you say, are you married then?"

"No."

"Why not?

"Because, until now it has been too early," he answers quietly.

I look at him from the side. His face looks too serious for the light tone of the driver's questions.

"You've got a beautiful woman! You should marry her, man, otherwise you'll lose her. You can marry here, more tourists do so. 'Jáman', no problem! Promise me you'll marry her this week."

"That I cannot promise," he says seriously.

It is late in the evening when we drive into the town, which consists of one main road with hotels and guest houses on either side. Everywhere loud music and many tourists. Doubtfully I look around. It is quite a contrast from the peaceful atmosphere we have left. We stop in front of the guest house where Hermod has made a reservation, a collection of wooden huts. The beach is behind. Reggae sounds loudly in the air. There turns out to be a concert next door tonight. This week is spring break for the American college students, that is why it is so crowded and there are concerts every night.

At the reception we get the key of a hut. The hut is dirty inside. There is one bed with a pale sheet, a small table with one chair and a wobbly cupboard. We put down our luggage and refresh ourselves at the nearby toilets. After a snack we close the door and plump down on the bed. The reggae drones through the thin wooden walls. Somewhat discouraged I look around.

"Welcome to the world," he says softly.

Jamaica, Negril, March

It is night. The reggae drones through my head. Everything itches, it seems as if there are fleas, or otherwise I've been bitten by mosquitos. In my agitation I need to go to the toilet several times, which is quite a trek. The toilets are dirty. On my return I am accosted and chased by a drunken Jamaican. I feel pitiful and I am fed up with this. I long for our paradise. I do not feel like being in a crowded tourist resort at all. If we spend a week like this, I shall be broken when we go home.

Hermod is sleeping quietly beside me. He can sleep everywhere and at any time. Because of his irregular duties at the medical emergency service, he is well trained in this. His chest goes up and down. I envy him his relaxation. Towards four o'clock in the morning the concert ends. Drunken people are stumbling noisily past our hut. I sneak to the toilet once more and cool my frustration under a cold shower.

Back in bed a bit later he starts to snore loudly. That is all that was missing! I think laughingly. A wave of tenderness sweeps over me.

"Je snurkt, schat," ("You're snoring love,") I softly whisper in Dutch.

It becomes silent.

Maybe he understands Dutch better in his sleep? I get more cheerful. Ah, I am making a fuss about nothing. During the day we can look for a better place to stay. In the travel guide Negril was said to be an attractive town, maybe this is just the worst part. If it turns out to be really horrible, we can always go back. Besides, the scuba diving course will determine the tone of the coming days anyway.

He starts snoring again, even louder now.

"Misschien moet je op je zij gaan liggen?" ("Maybe you should lie on your side?") I whisper again in Dutch.

Very softly he whispers in his sleep:

"I don't understand what you're saying..."

He does not wake up, the snoring stops however. I cannot hold my laughter. Softly I crawl towards him and finally, slowly fall asleep.

In the morning I tell him of my nightly hardships. He shows the right concern about all the little discomforts and gets indignant about me being chased by the drunken man.

"We'll go and see what it looks like in daylight and inquire about the diving school. We can look for another guest house. If everything turns out to be really horrible, we can still go back tomorrow and spend the last days in our paradise."

I feel entirely understood and supported.

"I always used to sleep in this kind of establishment, or just under the open sky. Now this doesn't appeal to me any more, I prefer a bit of comfort, at least some hygiene. A tent in nature is fine as well. Could this be because we're getting older?" I wonder aloud.

"I've also stayed overnight in the most primitive places while travelling. I know that experience very well, now I also enjoy a bit more comfort. It's experience, I think, it hasn't got anything to do with growing older."

I prefer to think he's right.

When I tell him about our Dutch/English exchange concerning

his snoring he looks at me roguishly.

"Did I say that? That was cuuuuuuute!"

In a much better mood we set off on our way. We walk over the beach to where restaurants and terraces are situated. Reggae sounds everywhere, though not so deafening any more. Some Jamaicans are jogging with graceful bouncing steps along the water line. The atmosphere is easy-going. It is the same Jamaica, but more worldly. The sun is shining, the ocean is blue and we still like reggae. We find a sympathetic terrace under a few palmtrees with an ocean view and decide to have breakfast.

"Actually it isn't so bad here after all," I think aloud, enjoying my fruit salad and a cup of tea.

He sits relaxedly sprawled looking around.

"Not at all, to many people this is paradise. Look how many people come here to enjoy. But we're coming out of another paradise. It's just a sort of culture shock. But I feel at home here."

After a while we walk back to where we have seen an advertisement for a diving school. The diving school is called 'The Dolphin Divers', so that should be okay! We talk to two friendly girls, who give us information about the course. We can start the same day studying theory. We shall get a private teacher and we can determine our own pace for the coming days. They recommend a quiet and welcoming guest house, on the other side of the road. As far as I am concerned the choice has been made, but the Hermod-way is first to investigate all possibilities thoroughly, so we say we shall probably come back later.

The recommended guest house is beyond expectations. It is a big white house, with balconies and in the back yard there is another building in the same style and a smaller, white wooden cottage.

A dark young man, with a warm, open smile, introduces himself as John and shows us several beautiful, clean rooms with bathroom attached, for the same reasonable price as the place where we have just spent the night. The Elleke-way, would be to get our luggage, sign up at the Dolphin Divers and start studying in the course book on the beach. However for his peace of mind we follow the Hermod-way and say that we shall probably come back later. We look at three other guest houses and one and a half hours later we choose John's place anyway. We get our luggage and settle down to organising our new room in the cottage.

We are very content. He is especially content, because now he knows for sure that we have made the best choice. I am happy to allow him this pleasure.

While I arrange our new household, unpack our things and organise the room, he quietly lies on the bed watching me. Suddenly he pulls me close tenderly, but purposefully. His hands disappear in between the folds of my sarong.

"You probably don't feel like having a shower together?" he whispers.

"Hmm, ... now you're saying so, actually I do."

Later we lie intertwined on the bed again.

We intertwine in our souls.

For a long time we remain silent, both impressed by the magnitude of this intimacy.

Later we walk in the direction of the beach. While he goes to check whether the other diving school he had in mind is no better than the Dolphin Divers, I go and have a swim, a sunbathe and catch up with some sleep. Half an hour later he returns. The choice has fallen on the Dolphin Divers. We sign up, make an appointment for the first theory session the next morning and receive the course book to study the first chapters in advance. The rest of the afternoon we spend swimming, sunbathing, and studying on the beach.

Late afternoon people are gathering on the beach to watch the sunset, for we are on the western side of the island. When the last red glow disappears behind the horizon and the sky turns from orange and purple into mauve and dark greyish blue, peace descends.

When it gets too dark to read, we walk along the beach. He puts his arm around me.

"It was a very beautiful and special love making we had this afternoon," he says.

I nod: "And there have been more, these weeks... and before too."

"Yes."

We stop at a restaurant under thick foliage, with round wooden tables in the shifting sand. This looks like our place for this evening. Amiably we share a dish and conversation turns to the job in London. While our talk of the future gets more detailed, we also discuss other possibilities, like living in Norway. All kinds of practicalities are involved, which he has a hard time dealing with. In his own environment this seems to be even harder for him.

Once he said: "I'm not a practical man, you know, it took me six years to buy a fridge and still I haven't got one."

Since then this pronouncement has been symbolic for his attitude towards practical matters.

"... and considering that fridge, I'll buy it, this will take me only an hour or two. The only thing is that it might not be the perfect fridge you have in mind," I joke.

"No, you'll probably buy one that makes noise, I would never be able to live with that."

"You'll have to accept that. Some things we'll do the Hermod-way, other things we'll do the Elleke-way, but since you've mentioned the problem, I can watch out for noisy fridges."

Relaxed we sit together. It is a rich feeling, we love each other and life is open to us. Those practicalities, we shall get through.

Quietly we walk back along the beach and pass several campfires and playing bands. Here and there we stand to listen and swing. He records some music with his small tape recorder, which he uses to keep an account of his travels.

Next morning we have breakfast on a terrace at the beach and study on together. At a certain point I lay down my book, look around at the blue sea, the palm trees, the colours, the relaxed faces of the people and sigh:

"It has been very good these weeks."

"Yes, and it still is... But I realize there have been difficult moments too, which I'm mainly responsible for. I have realized that sometimes I'm just trying to dominate you. You are strong and take a lot of space. Sometimes I've been resisting that. I want to have everything under control, be the strongest, get all attention and all energy. In my other relationships I have dominated too, more than I do with you, but you are able to deal with it."

"I know I sometimes take a lot of space, but with your help I'll learn to get over this habit. I need some time to learn to give you space. Now and then we'll struggle with our personalities... but the way we get through these time and again, gives a lot of trust. We'll grow through it."

"Yes," he says casually, "the unit that we are now, needs some adjustments here and there."

"That you say beautifully..."

"It's how it is; you and I are now a unit together, and this unit needs some adjustments."

Then I have to laugh:

"These adjustments may take ten or twenty years, but who cares, as long as the beautiful moments outweigh."

At ten o' clock we report to the diving school, where we meet Sven, our instructor. It clicks between the three of us. In the shadow of a roofed terrace, over a piña colada and a banana drink, we fill in some forms and get a lecture and a test about the first chapters of the book. The second session is followed by a first dive in the swimming pool. Great fun with the first exercises under water.

In the afternoon Hermod carries me around in the sea and I

am hanging in his arms like a baby. The little child is allowed to be free. Never before have I so totally surrendered to anybody. I feel nurtured by his love with each vessel of my being. I feel him deeply within me.

"Now I want to carry you."

With some effort, and supported by the lifting force of the salt water, I can just hold him, double folded, in my arms. For a long, long time I rock him gently through the water, like a mother her child.

Now the child in him is allowed to be free. I see something unfolding within him, as if something is opening which has been locked up for a long time.

I feel his strength and his purity, I feel his core. For a long, long time it is silent. Then he says with a small voice:

"I want a coconut rum, with a straw."

"Oh, I thought you'd want warm, sweet mother's milk."

"Mmmmm."

Gently I let go of him.

"You know, you're a very challenging man. Sometimes you get the hidden shadow sides out of me, which have always been there, but which I wasn't aware of. Through you I can see and transform them. But you also get the best out of me, beautiful sides, as I've always hoped I could be. The best and the worst, all together quite a potential."

"To me you're a most challenging woman. With you I also meet my worst sides, well, otherwise I come across them anyway, ..."

"And your best sides?"

"Yes, those too, ... and that's a new experience. This whole relationship is a new experience to me..." he says thoughtfully.

"I still have the feeling we can bring each other to God, I have had this since the beginning of our relationship. I really don't know what it means, but this is how it feels. When I look at you, I see the divine, as if I'm looking through different dimensions."

"You're the one here who is vèry special."

We look at each other and slowly we step out of the water.

The next day, after the diving instruction, we take a long walk along the beach. We pass idyllic secluded places, with some palm trees and reed huts. Towards sunset we arrive at a small wooden bar, with a swing in a palm tree. While swinging and sipping a tequila we watch the sunset. We find a characteristic terrace along the tide line, some chairs and tables under palms, paper lanterns and a bright star sky. It is an evening of untold stories. At some point, when he tells about when he was 17. I get a strange awareness of time.

"At that time I was a tiny little girl, like Imre..."

"You see, all I had to do was wait!"

I burst out laughing. When he got to know the children, he was so fond of Imre, who was still a tiny toddler, that he joked: "I'll stay with you until I can marry her."

"The past has been. More than ever before I'm living in the present... with you. The children are also in the present, as a result of the past, but they fit into this present. I feel like a young girl with her first love, fresh and new. You are my great love, it's as if it has never been otherwise. I'm so grateful we're together."

He lays his hand on my arm and looks at me lovingly:

"Me too."

In the dark night we walk the long way back. A star is falling, we stand still. Silently I wish that our love may be fulfilling for all our life, and that from our love we may draw nourishment and inspiration to share with others. A deep trust and knowing comes over me. Our love is and will be and it transcends time. It is good as it is.

I see him folding his hands and have the feeling his wish is of a similar kind. With arms around each other we continue, but then I stop him:

"I need to hold you for a moment!"

We stay in a long embrace and reach out to the stars. We are transparent.

"I love you." He says it softly and earnestly.

I love you, I answer without words. I feel him inside like I feel myself, there is oneness. Silence.

"You're so beautiful in all your sarongs!... And your breasts are looking so inviting."

He touches them gently. I come back to earth.

"I'm not so aware of that."

"That doesn't show, since you're walking and moving around so freely and elegantly."

"Hmm, something has opened up during these weeks. I feel free and not insecure any more. Thanks to you and the sun and the sea and the wind. I feel... me."

We walk further.

"You know, London or Norway, if it is Norway, I hope the circumstances will help a bit, your radio programme, finding a house. We just need a bit of luck. It might all go very smoothly, when we trust within."

He pulls me close and and says softly:

"The only thing I need is a bit of courage."

"There's no hurry, when we follow the natural course of things, the right time will come, it will ripen within and it won't be a matter of courage any more. It's good the way it is between us now."

The answer is a gentle pinch.

At home we take a bath, to wash off the salt. The plug does not fit well. A long time after all the water has disappeared, we are still in the bath.

The next day we have our first dive in the ocean. A new world opens up to us, a silent world of colourful fish, purple, blue, golden yellow, green - no human being can invent this - woods of coral, weeds and anemones. Weightlessly we float above the coral, now and then looking at each other, gesturing everything is okay. We share our wonder. This is what I have always wished for, I realize. It is happening here, now, the two of us together in this wonderful world.

In the afternoon I take a walk on my own and buy some presents and clothes for the children. We arrange to meet up later in the afternoon. It is the last but one day... And I am not looking forward to leaving all this behind and being without him for some time. It does not fit any more to be without each other. We talk about his visit in April. He will stay for a couple of weeks then. We make plans for Yoram's birthday and other things and then we rest a bit. He writes a card, his only card these holidays, to Vidar, his best friend.

The sun is almost setting.

I fetch a piña colada, which we share. We lie on a sun lounger on the beach. He is a bit irritated by two American college students, who are lying behind us and making critical comments about the passers-by. Briskly he stands up, to lie down a bit further away. I do not care about those students, but I follow him. I watch him from the side. He is beautiful, but when he is angry he can also look like a rag. He is getting a bit grey at the temples, which I find quite attractive. Though he does not want to hear about getting older. It tickles inside.

"You're getting a bit grey, love, we shouldn't wait too long with our little one, otherwise he'll think you're his grandpa."

"Hmm, if he or she thinks so, then he or she has no concept of timelessness."

"Well, that will be okay, for of course he or she'll get a timeless education."

"Would you want to manipulate our child?" he asks quasi indignant.

3

The Scream

A flash
A scream
A bang
two ruptured hearts

Silence

The world stands still
time stops
inside
the scream lasts
and lasts
echoing
through the universe

The last day. It rains in the daytime for the first time since we have been in Jamaica. A tropical shower. It patters in streams on the big leaves of the banana tree in front of our guest house. Sitting on the veranda, with our study books in front of us we discuss how to structure the day. He does not feel ready for the test and decides to postpone it until tomorrow morning, before we go to the airport. He wants to study in the morning and the evening, this afternoon we shall have our last dive in the sea. We also have to go to the bank to get money in order to pay John for the last nights. I become a bit irritated. I want to complete the diving course today, so I shall take the test today. I would like to make something special of this last evening. Besides, I do not like last days.

"It isn't our last day," he says in a friendly way, "tomorrow we'll have a lovely flight together and in April I'll come again, and..."

"... And we'll have a whole life together," I add.

"Yes, ... and also after this life!" he says seriously.

I give him a hug:

"You are right. I shouldn't make it difficult, as if this is the last day of our life. I think I'm a bit nervous about the test, in fact, I know it. Instead of studying I'll do some therapeutic work and repair my bag."

"Who knows, maybe there will be some time tonight to do something together. But for me it's not so important, we've had so many special evenings and moments. Now, I'm still saturated with that beautiful evening the day before yesterday."

He concentrates on his book again and I sit silently repairing my shoulderbag. It is a cosy household, father a book, mother her needlework.

Hermod goes to John to call in order to arrange transport to Kingston. I listen for a while. He is very good at getting things done and getting the best help from people. With his deep, warm voice, his open interest, with his flair, tact and humour, he captivates a lot of people, even by telephone. Finally he manages to arrange that our ticket, which is valid from Kingston, will be altered free of charge to Montego Bay, which is nearby. This saves us hours of travelling and a lot of money.

I walk to the diving school and take my test. It is like a test paper at highschool. When I am finished I do not understand why I have been so tense about it. Afterwards we drive to the cliffs. We go to a small cove in between the rocks and dive into the water. First the exercises, we rescue each other from all kinds of dangers. Which is difficult for me, because he is so tall.

"I suddenly realize I won't be able to save you from all possible dangers," I say to him, breathing heavily, while pulling him through the water and trying to hold his head above the surface.

He laughs.

Yet I manage.

Then we go on an exploration trip along the reef.

Okay? Okay! we signal. Through our masks we see each other radiating. I stand on my hands on the sea bottom and make a few somersaults. We take each other's hands and make a stretched somersault together. We kiss, swim hand in hand and I lie on his back, letting myself be pulled by him.

The landscape is almost surrealistic, with fans and big grooved balls of coral. Fish watch us quietly and a big sea-eel sticks its head out of its cave. I see a small, glowing shell in the sand and put it in my swimsuit. He picks up something too. For a while I swim on my back, looking at the light surface far above us. Life on shore seems far away. Everything moves here slowly back and forth in an eternal flow, the uterus of the world. We dance and float just above the bottom of the sea.

Then Sven is waiting for us and gestures that we are going back. We have a break and replace our tanks for a second dive. Hermod is happy.

"That was great to float like that in neutral buoyancy and to be able to regulate this by breathing; breathe in and up we go, breathe out and down we go!" He spreads his arms and dances around. "I love that term: neutral buoyancy, one should be able to maintain this in the stream of life as well and allow yourself to go along with the flow! And all those fishes quietly continue their pursuits and look at us so amicably."

We make a second dive. For me the course has been completed now. He makes an appointment to take his last test tomorrow.

In the car we sit contentedly next to each other. We show each other our treasures. He has found two loose pieces of coral and a big elegantly shaped shell. I have my small mother-of-pearl-glowing shell, as a symbolic pearl of this journey. Many times I take it out again, happy as a child.

"Very beautiful!" he nods reassuringly.

He manages to arrange our transport to the airport tomorrow with the driver who drives us back to the diving school.

When we have rinsed our scuba gear and refreshed ourselves at our guest house we go out to have lunch. Our favourite table at our favourite stand is occupied. He gets restless. When we are about to settle for the restaurant next door, he hesitates.

"This is nothing either!"

Then he wants to go back to our usual stand, but to another table. We look at the menu, he chooses an omelette and I order a delicious lobster salad. I look at his profile. Still irritated about the occupied table, he stares at the sea. Suddenly he seems to see beyond the horizon, his face lightens up and he starts to radiate:

"These weeks have been so wonderful and timeless, here in this paradisical environment... and the way it is between us. This is how it is and it will always be like this. What there is between us now goes beyond time and space... You have always been trying to convince me that life can be so beautiful. Now I'm starting to believe you. Never before have I been so close to paradise. And if I were to die right now, I wouldn't mind, for now I know how beautiful life can be."

"Ah, this summer you also said that you wouldn't mind dying after the beautiful weeks we'd had together, and what wonderful experiences we've had since then! Life can be beyond our imagination, like you always say yourself."

'Beyond imagination' is a winged expression between us. The first time he used it was on a grey rainy morning on the west coast of Norway, some time ago. A solitary dolphin has been spotted there, which occasionally seeks interaction with humans. On the evening we arrived we heard that the dolphin had been away without a trace for a long time. The next morning I did not feel well, the weather was dreary and I did not feel like starting the day. He took me in his arms and said gently:

"This day could be beyond our imagination!"

The sun started to shine. At the harbour we discovered the dolphin waiting for us and we shared an experience of extraordinary intimacy, by which we were completely lifted up. We stayed in the icy water for such a long time that afterwards I could not get warm. He wrapped me in woollen blankets and put me in the car turning the engine and the heater on. But it had been beyond our imagination and we were so touched that the rest of that day we only had to look at each other to get tears in our eyes...

"Yes, but then I wonder, why can't everyone be so happy? Why can't everyone afford a holiday like this, why is this reserved only for a minority of humanity? And why are we part of it? I want everybody to experience paradise!"

"Remember that dream I had when I was ill? In it I was conscious of all the human suffering on earth and that I didn't want to be here any more... Immediately this was followed by an expansion of my consciousness, in which I experienced space and light, contained the suffering and got insight at the same time. At soul level we are free from suffering. It is a part of us which suffers, our human instrument, which needs adjustment. This suffering is real, our freedom from suffering as well, or maybe even more real, in another reality. We don't have to feel guilty in our privileged society. All of us can't go into developmental projects or go to war areas to help. However we can - and this is our responsibility - contribute in other ways. We can easily transfer some money to one or other charity, or with a little more effort, prepare a pack with clothes, food and a cuddly toy for war children. But most of all we can take responsibility for the way in which we lead our own lives. By leading our life in fullness, with our heart, in love, without defences and selfmade restrictions. With this we make a contribution to our environment and to the universe. We can express our unique essence and stimulate others to do the same."

He nodds: "In our relationship both of us have often experienced a creative input. Now it is time for a creative output."

We review all kinds of ideas about a fulfilled life together; travelling here and there, networking, writing, teaching workshops and seminars, a lecture he has been invited to give by a professor. He decides to accept the invitation and to give that lecture after all.

"Now I feel ashamed that I made such a fuss about that occupied table."

"Isn't that human? I feel ashamed that I made such a fuss this morning, because I was set on spending this day nicely together."

"Sometimes I want to wake up everybody and take them to paradise and sometimes I don't care at all."

"I don't believe that, with your sensitivity, you, as a doctor. I know how concerned you are in your work. I see how you deal with people. You radiate such a lot of love. You rather care too much, that's why you sometimes block yourself out of all feelings."

He frowns: "Sometimes I feel nothing, only ugliness."

"I see a lot of beauty in you."

"I'm a beautiful, ugly man."

"The ugliness is included in the beauty."

"Now we're talking here about wonderful ideals and ideas, but when I'm back home in my apartment, I'm afraid that I'll fall back into my old rooted patterns and maybe I won't be able to get out of my bed again."

"When you fall back now, after all that has happened, then I won't wait until we have found a house. I'll take my children and my stuff and we'll come at once to bring your life into uproar."

He smiles.

"I had a special dream last night: We drove together with Jenka in the car through a town and we're looking for something... It feels as if the dream means something, but I don't know what."

I ponder on it. Jenka is his late dog, who appears more often in his dreams when something important is about to happen. She represents to him trust and unconditional love. This is present between us. Maybe Jenka leads us somewhere in his dream?

"Do you know what we were looking for? How was the atmosphere?"

"The atmosphere was good, quiet and relaxed, but what we were looking for, I don't know. The town looked a bit like Oslo and felt like home, although we were unknown there. We didn't know the way, but were very relaxed."

"Hmm, interesting."

We get the bill. I am astonished by it. I had misread the price of the lobster salad, which turns out to be three times as expensive as I thought.

"I had noticed, but I decided not to say anything. I thought maybe you wanted to splash out and enjoy, because it's the last day."

"How sweet of you, I have enjoyed it very much, but if I had known this, I would never have chosen it."

"Then it was an expensive and delicious human mistake."

He goes home to study and I walk along the beach to the centre of town, to the bank. The cash dispenser does not accept my card, there turns out to be a malfunction today. It is dark by now. I know he wants me to walk back along the main road, but I hate these cars racing by and I prefer walking along the lonely beach. In order to get there I have to pass through a slum area and I am accosted repeatedly. A white woman should not walk here on her own, my logical mind says, but actually I am enjoying it. A smell of hashish fills the air and reggae sounds from small radios. When I arrive at the silent beach, I am relieved anyway. Firmly I step along the tide line and splash into the water.

Once at home he asks why I am so late and why didn't I take a taxi, and didn't I even walk back along the main road, but along the beach on my own? He is outraged at my recklessness. I see his concern, which touches me.

While he studies I repair my repairs to my bag.

"Are you in therapy again?"

"No," I say smilingly, "I don't need therapy any more. I feel free and happy. But this afternoon the zipper broke down and it's such a fine bag, it deserves some care."

Together we read on the bed. I read a piece in the Pathwork*, about inner blockages, which may show up in an intimate relationship. This causes friction, but also offers a chance to work things out. I ask him whether he wants to hear it. He wants to.

"Hmm, still you surprise me again and again by the way you are able to deal with my moods. You are really incredible."

"Ah, in that event on the beach I really was a tiny little girl."

"Yes, then I could have reached out to you, but at that moment I couldn't come up with it."

"These weeks I have come to respect you even more than before. I have seen more of your shadow sides and I have discovered that I can learn a lot from it, considering my own shadow sides. And I have seen more of your beautiful sides, from which I learn the most and by which I'm completely delighted. I admire your sharp and creative mind, you inspire me and lift me up. And above all I feel your love."

"You're spoiling me, then you risk that I keep on misbehaving and then I'm afraid that I won't do you any good."

"Don't worry. I see that you're doing your utmost in everything. As soon as I have the feeling that you're not doing me any good, I'll warn you fairly in advance, but thus far I'm growing and flourishing with you. Never before have I been so happy. It's as if you've put my spine straight. I feel open, naked and free. It's as if we undress in front of each other gradually and drop all our defences."

He does not answer, but looks at me straight and silently. We look at each other and inside each other.

I read out another piece on transcending duality - one of our favourite topics. Passionately he sets forth his ideas. According to him it is the art of accepting and containing both polarities, the positive and the negative, light and dark, joy and sorrow, love and hate. To walk a narrow middle path and to transcend to a state of consciousness which is beyond duality. He does not want to speak any more in terms of positive and negative. Thus far I go along with him.

Our point of difference is that I think we can manifest this state of transcendent consciousness here in life on earth, for which a constructive intention is needed. Consciousness is light, in my opinion. He is not certain about this and thinks this is a judgement in duality.

In the heat of his argument I watch him and listen to him. I feel it is important what he says. Verbally he is very gifted and I cannot always match him. Besides I am distracted by looking at him. These weeks he has come to be very good looking, sun tanned, vital and completely in his strength, as I have not seen him before. Something has happened to him during these weeks too, something has opened up inside him. He sits on the bed in his shorts, with bare, tanned breast and shoulders. His brown hair is wild, his face unshaved and his eyes fire blue sparks. Like a Norwegian god, but a radiant one this time. For a moment I feel tempted to take my camera, but I do not want to interrupt the discussion. So I take a hypnotic picture, as he once taught me. I close my eyes for an instant and imprint his image on my retina.

"I see your point and I don't have any reply to it now. But I stay with the viewpoint that in the end it is about manifesting this state of being beyond duality here and do something with it on earth."

I am tired. It is ten o'clock. Tomorrow we have a long journey ahead of us. My bags are packed. All his stuff is still spread around.

"I'll pack tonight, in the bathroom, so that you can sleep quietly. Shall we go for a swim now?"

I hesitate for a moment, I am really tired, but it is also a fine conclusion.

"Okay."

I am looking forward to it, with our previous nightly swimming parties in memory. We take our towels and go outside. The warm evening air envelopes us as a soft velvet blanket. Crickets and tree frogs are singing. Silently we walk next to each other down the entrance lane of the guest house, each of us still in thoughts about our discussion. I am aware of the dynamic between us, which is positively charged, sparks fly back and forth. We arrive at the main road and keep to the right, because there is the access to the beach.

"I enjoy opposing you a little bit in these kind of dialogues, to emphasize the polarity," I say.

"Yes, so do I," he says warmly.

"... while I feel at a deeper level we are completely in line with each other," I complete my sentence.

He looks aside, touches my shoulder and opens his mouth to say something.

Suddenly headlights show up on the left behind us. By now we are in the middle of the road. I take one step back. He runs three steps forward to pass before the car.

This can't be done, it's a miscalculation. I realize and I feel that he realizes this at the same time.

The car races by and I hear a muffled bang.

In a flash I see he is being hit, he must be hit.

I feel his shock, my shock.

I hear a long icy scream... coming out of my own mouth.

Inside something is tearing apart.

Right in front of me a shadow is standing on the other side of the road... it is not him.

Much further ahead, about 50 metres, something drops on the road.

I run towards it...

It seems an eternity.

There he lies. A lifeless heap, as a child lying on his side.

When I reach him, something inside me registers: this is very serious. Something inside me registers how his lower leg is lying at a broken angle, how his nose is broken, a pool of blood is developing, though I'm unclear yet where it is coming from. His eyes are closed, the right eye is damaged. Blood is streaming out of his head, but also from his side. His chest must be damaged severely. He is not breathing. I kneel at his side and feel his pulse, no pulse...

"This can't be, this can't be, this can't be! Come back, please come back. After all we have been going through, after all we have discussed, all we have chosen, you can't leave me now! Come back, my love, come back. You have to come back!"

Someone sits down beside me, a man, a foreigner. He says he is a doctor, and feels his pulse. He turns him somewhat on his back and feels his chest.

"This is very serious," he says.

He gives me instructions for resuscitation. He insufflates and I press on his chest, while I keep repeating: "Come back, love, please come back!"

I keep saying: "This can't be, this isn't possible..."

I see something happening in his being, a struggle, as if his soul makes an attempt to react. He is out of consciousness, but I can feel he hears me.

Do I have the right to call you back? With all this damage, what kind of life could be possible for you? You would never want to live with a severe handicap. But I stay with you. I believe in miracles. I am willing to believe that everything is possible, until the opposite is proven.

"Please, come back..."

Then something inside me becomes aware of something, his soul, his essence withdrawing from his body. His face becomes peaceful.

Something inside me experiences him standing beside me and lying his hand on my shoulder. Something inside me surrenders to the inevitable.

But another part of me is desperate:

"This can't be, it can't be!"

The man beside me stops insufflating:

"This is no use, he is dead. He isn't reacting at all."

And he disappears out of my sight.

There is a lot of turmoil around us, a crowd has gathered, there is a lot of noise, but I hardly notice. People are addressing me, asking me whether he is my husband, whether I know him.

I do not answer. It has happened. All the rest is of no importance.

I am sitting there kneeling down in my sarong on the street beside him, my arm around him, stroking his hair with my other hand. I feel an overwhelming love. And an overwhelming, incomprehensible emptiness, and dull pain, disrupting pain. This is not possible.

Time passes.

I don't know how long I am sitting there, touching, caressing his body, trying to grasp what has happened.

While another part of me is conscious of his presence, beside me, behind me, around me, caressing me and being dazed himself as well.

I expect an ambulance to come at any moment, so that we can be taken to a hospital. Somewhere I am still hoping for a miracle to happen. But nothing happens, apart from a number of people around me, making a lot of fuss.

A policeman addresses me. He is asking me a lot of questions. Is that my husband? What has happened? Where am I staying?

I answer his questions and ask about the ambulance.

"It's coming," he says, making notes.

There are more policemen. Nobody does anything. A man approaches me with tears in his eyes.

"Oh, Ma'am", he says with an American accent, "I saw it all happening. I was standing on the side of the road where you crossed. Oh, Ma'am, I think it's so terrible."

I realize he was the shadow I saw on the other side of the road, which I took to be Hermod, for an instant, when the car raced by. We look at each other. I lay my hand on his shoulder for a moment and say nothing. There are more people, Jamaicans and tourists, who address me and show their sympathy. I say nothing and kneel down again at his body. It has already become cold and stiff.

He is really dead.

Suddenly I feel terribly lost in the crowd and ask somebody to fetch John. I point to our guest house, not even 100 metres away. Another policeman comes and asks questions, the same questions. Shortly I repeat that this is my partner, he was knocked down by a car, and I ask again about the ambulance.

Time passes, timeless time, nothing happens, there is only chaos.

More than once I ask for someone to get John. Another policeman asks more questions. For my answers I refer him to the previous policeman and ask him what is going to happen. He does not know, or at least he seems unclear about it.

Finally there is John. His face shows terror. I stand up.

"John, help me, nobody is doing anything, ask them where's the ambulance, what's going to happen."

Another policeman has some answers. No ambulance, but a car will come to take him to the mortuary, he says. They need his passport. I can hardly believe it. No ambulance? Just carry him off to a mortuary? What kind of nightmare is this?

We wait, nothing happens.

No one can tell me how long it will take until the car arrives. I realize something has to happen. I have to call Norway, Holland. All kind of things will need to be arranged. I need to fetch his passport and maybe things for myself to take with me to the mortuary. Maybe I cannot call from there. It is not always possible to call to Europe.

"John, I need to get his passport and I need to make some phone calls."

"You can call from my place, I'm going with you."

I tell the nearest policeman what I am going to do and point to John's guest house.

"I'm there, let me know when the car arrives and don't take him away before I'm back."

He agrees. To be sure I tell the same to another policeman. I ask John whether they will do what I ask them. He says so and addresses another policeman as well. I take another glance at his body.

I have to leave you for a little while, my love. I need to arrange some things, let your family know what has happened. I'll be back soon.

Hand in hand John and I walk back to the guest house. I feel Hermod walking on my other side, he takes my hand. I feel his hand in mine and at the same time I see my physical hand hanging at my side. I cannot grasp it.

"I need your help now John. I absolutely don't know what to do."

"I'll help you, I'm there for you. "

I feel how much he means it. I feel how close we stand together as human beings.

"We are friends for life, aren't we?"

"Yes."

We walk up the entrance lane of the guest house. An hour ago Hermod and I walked down it... still filled with the talk we had had, filled with the day, with each other, with everything...

"We were so happy together..." I say desperately.

"I know, I could see it."

We walk up the stairs to our room. With trembling hands I unlock the door.The room is just the way we left it. All Hermod's stuff is spread out on the bed. What do I need? My address book, to make the phone calls. His passport, my passport, they are in the main house with John. His insurance card. I have to change my clothes, I cannot spend the night in a mortuary in a sarong. John sits down on the bed. I get some things together and go to the bathroom to change my clothes. I need to pee.

While I am on the toilet I realize how absurd it is that my body just continues doing what it has to do, while his is lying there on the street. I start to feel more and more shaky, but I am still present. I look in the mirror. I see a living, sun tanned young woman, with wide, stern eyes.

I am alive, he is not any more. It is absurd, I do not want this. I do not want this!

I pack my shoulder bag, close the door and we go to John's home. He gets our passports and tickets. John's mother greets me with an embrace and tears in her eyes. John shows me the telephone and tells me it is possible to make three international calls per day. I take out my address book and look for the phone number of his brother, Jan Marcus. John dials the number of the operator. I give him Jan Marcus' number. There is a connection and he hands the receiver to me. It is 12 midnight, so it will be 6 o'clock in the morning over there. How shocking this will be for him.

Trrrrrt, ... trrrrrt, ... trrrrrrt...

"Hallo, det er Jan Marcus." ("Hello this is Jan Marcus")

He sounds awake.

"Jan Marcus, it's Elleke."

"Oh, hello, Elleke, how are you?"

He sounds surprised, friendly and a bit uncertain.

I take a deep breath, there is no way of saying this carefully.

"Hermod has just had an accident ..."

I sense his shock.

"Is it serious?"

I take another deep breath:

"He is dead."

For a moment it is silent on the other side of the line.

"No! No, oh, no!..."

He cries. And now I can cry as well. We are crying together. I see John on the opposite side on the couch crying as well.

"What happened?" he asks after some time.

I describe the accident and see it happening again before my eyes. It is incomprehensible, for both of us. I ask him whether he wants to hear something about the past weeks and briefly depict our experience of paradise, how happy we have been and Hermod's words of this afternoon. It is part of the story, it is important.

In the division of the moment I feel beside all pain and despair and bewilderment also gratitude. What has been, has been good. We cry and talk a bit more and agree that he will inform the family and call me back later, as it is so difficult to call from here. We exchange all relevant numbers and with difficult, we say goodbye.

When I put down the receiver I look at John.

"His family is my family, it has felt like that from the first moment I met them."

Now I call home, to speak to Peter. Despite the fact that he is being woken up he is fully present and concerned. I feel his support. He will inform the children, family and friends. I give him the phone number for the guest house and numbers for Hermod's family. So we can reach each other, like a circle over the world.

When I put down the receiver, John is still sitting there. He has not been able to follow this talk, for it took place in Dutch.

"That was Peter, my ex-partner. Our relationship has always been good. He will support me and the children wherever necessary."

The Norwegian and Dutch networks have been started. I feel less alone now I know that the people I love and the people he loves will soon know what has happened. Now I want to go back to him.

We walk back to the place of the accident. There are still a lot of people and policemen, but his body is gone. There is only a big dried puddle of blood on the road. I address a policeman and can hardly hide my anger. It was agreed that they would wait for me, they knew where I was. It turns out that he was taken away just a few minutes ago and they would not have let me go in the car to the mortuary anyway. And I would not have been allowed to stay there overnight. At most I would have been allowed to see him for a few minutes. At 8 am I will be expected at the police station and then I shall be able to see him. All this is reported to me very calmly.

I cannot stand it. I want to be with him for the rest of the night or at least I had wanted to say goodbye to him. I left him on the assumption that it would be for a little while. The policeman repeats himself once more. John, who has heard this, offers to drive me to the mortuary, so that I can see him for a while. It is a one and a half hour drive, back and forth.

I hesitate. I want to be with him, but he is not in his body any more. I do feel responsible for what they do with his body and yet I still want to say goodbye to it. It is 1 am. Suddenly I feel how tired I am. There will be more dreadful hours and days, weeks...

I look at John. It is a shock for him as well, all of what is happening. Maybe it is better to try to get some rest, although rest..... there still needs a lot to be arranged. I don't know any more. I feel guilty towards Hermod.

The policeman is unmoved. He repeats that I shall be expected at 8 am at the police station and that he needs Hermod's passport and ticket now. Suddenly I see that this is a human being as well, trying to carry out his profession. No matter how in-human he may seem to me right now. I decide to stay here and apologise for my anger, tell him that I am a bit upset and that I understand that they are just doing their job. But what am I apologising for? It is ridiculous what is happening here and I think I am allowed to be more than a bit upset.

With difficulty I hand over his passport and ticket.

John and I walk back to the guest house.

"I shouldn't have left him, I'd wanted to stay with him," I say desperately.

"No, you've done the right thing. You had to call his family, you shouldn't feel guilty about that," he reassures me. "They shouldn't have taken him away!"

Again I have the feeling that Hermod is walking on my other side. I have not left him, for he is not there any more. He is here, with me. It is hard to grasp.

John suggests that I will probably depart later. But I realize that if possible, I will try to take my flight home and get Hermod's body on the first plane to Norway. I cannot fly with him all the way to Norway anyway, for we are on a different booking. I have to fly home first and from Holland I can fly to Norway as soon as possible. I want to go home, away from this hell. There is packing to do. But now I need some rest. I am trembling and exhausted.

"I thank you for supporting me like this," I say.

"That goes without saying. From the beginning when I saw you two, I felt connected with you both. And when I looked at you, I felt something stirring in my heart."

"We immediately felt connected with you too."

"It's terrible what is happening now."

We go to our, no, my room. Once inside, John leans against the wall and starts to cry. It comes out of his toes. I lean against his back and cry with him. Then David, his brother knocks on the door, to say there is a call, from Norway.

In the house I see John's mother pottering around. This whole family is being deprived of their nightly rest. As we walk to the telephone I murmur that I'm sorry for burdening them like this.

But they do not want to hear about it.

It is Cathrine, his youngest sister. Tears again. We don't have to say so much, she has heard everything from Jan Marcus. I tell her that Hermod's body has been taken away to the mortuary, that I have to be at the police station at eight o'clock. I ask her whether she will ask the others, Peter too, to call back early in the morning, or at noon Jamaican time, to discuss other things.

Now I really want some rest. John says I should not be alone now, he will stay with me tonight. It is well meant, but I need to be alone. And I can convince him of that. He will wake me at 6.30am.

I go to my room and lock the door.

Finally I'm alone. Though I feel I am not alone. I feel Hermod's presence almost physically. Then I see his appearance sitting on the bed and looking at me. I feel it more than I see it, it is a seeing-feeling. It does not surprise me, I am too shocked by everything to be surprised at anything right now. It is how it is. Only now I have some peace and quiet to allow this, to be with him.

He is doing fine. I can feel it in everything. It is as if he has been going through a lot during these past hours. He radiates rest and acceptance and I feel his love going out to me.

"Oh, my love, I know you are here, I can feel you, I can see you. But I am so confused. Why, why did this happen? I know it went like you so often have wished for, but we were going to live together. What about me now? This afternoon you said it has been a wonderful, timeless time, and it still is, and it will always be this way, you said. This applies to you now, but not to me."

"How do you know?"

I hear him gently and almost mockingly asking in my mind.

"You are right, I don't know. I don't know anything any more, at this moment I acknowledge I don't know anything, I am in the 'wonder-state', you were always talking about. The state of the unknowing. You are where you have always wanted to be, in the state 'beyond'."

"I'm still there. And our relationship does continue. Everything I've said today remains valid. There is no death, there is no time, there's only reality. Our relationship continues in another reality, in timelesness."

I hear your voice in my mind, it sounds like you. It sounds real, it feels real. Am I imagining this? This is, of course, what I would like to hear.

He looks at me straight and raises his finger. It sounds clear, insisting and lovingly:

"You were always the one who was trying to convince me there is another reality we can open up to. Now you shouldn't doubt yourself, you have to believe me. I am there and this is the only way we can be together now."

Only you can say it like that. It feels so real, deep inside I know this is reality. In any case, this is my reality. But I have a sceptical mind, although less sceptical than you had... have, no: had.

Now it sounds as if you know, without hesitatation. I am a psychologist, I know how people can create illusions for themselves. On the other hand, I also know that we humans create our own reality with our mind.

A saying by the Buddha, we have so often talked about this. This is my reality. I feel you, I see you, I know it is you. And if it is an illusion, then at least it is a valuable one, a consoling one.

"I feel you everywhere inside and around me. Remember, you said this to me, on our first night together? It was like that, it has more often been like that, now it is more like that than ever before. You are closer than ever. And still I want to be with you. I don't want live here on earth without you. When I think of what could have been, all our ideas for the future... I'm so sad. It hurts so incredibly. I'd rather die with you. For me it has finished here, it has been completed. Yet, at the same time I feel that, after all our talks about the essence of life, I have to go for this essence, for it has not changed by your death.

"As long as I live, life is worth living, whether it'll be short or long. I still feel love, love for the children, the people around me, and I feel our love. I'm so grateful for all that has been between us, and still is."

"...and will be..."

"Yes, and will be. Now I see too that we are connected forever, in timelessness."

"You have healed my life..."

"And you have healed mine. We have brought each other to surrender. It is good the way it is. Only I have no idea what this implies for me."

"Don't worry now. I'll stay with you. I love you ..."

"I want to talk more with you, but I'm so tired. Also I feel words are not necessary any more. Now we can communicate without words. Help me, please, you're the one who is 'beyond' now, you have to guide me. Now I need rest, you have your well-deserved rest, my love. You have lived, you have given a lot to people. You have given a lot to me. 'Takk for alt. Jeg elsker deg.' I say in Norwegian. "Thanks for everything. I love you."

"...i like måte." "...that's mutual"

I cry and feel his arms caressing around me. Falling asleep is not possible, but I lie down for one and a half hours and feel calmer. We are more together than ever. It is as if I live in two realities at the same time, as if my consciousness is stretching out. I am inside him and around him. I feel that I support him by this, by being with him in his reality. I perceive light around him, there are other souls with him as well.

Around 5.30am I decide to pack his stuff, for I have no idea how long it will take at the police station, the mortuary and to make arrangements for all the practical matters. It seems best to me to make sure all our things are ready for leaving. I take a shower. Two nights ago we were standing here together enjoying this shower. I feel a stab of pain. I wash my hair with his shampoo and dry myself with his towel. I put on my black dress again, tonight I can put on my bodysuit and stockings underneath. This was supposed to be a triumphant feeling; to step into my stockings again, sun tanned and vital. There is nothing triumphant any more. I look in the mirror. Apart from very swollen frog eyes from all the crying, I still look normal, alive. I start packing his things.

Everything hurts, his toiletry, his clothes, which he was always so careful about. Everything still looks clean after three weeks in Jamaica. His small library... I find even more books than I had expected.

"Love, what a lot you brought with you! How am I ever going to get this into this giant backpack of yours? And now are you leaving me with your mess. You see, what happens when you postpone everything!"

Actually I have to laugh at the absurdity of the situation and I feel a wave of tenderness. In the plastic bags which he managed to stuff into my luggage on the way to Jamaica, I find a pile of Norwegian newspapers. Which he had been carrying with him all the time, without looking at them. He could never throw anything away.

"Sorry, love, but now I am going to throw them away."

I am chatting aloud like this. I am aware of his presence, but I cannot see him clearly right now, my attention is being claimed too much by practical matters. Which is paradoxical, for these are his things. It feels a bit uneasy to rummage in them and decide about them, while I can feel his presence around me.

Towards seven o'clock there is a knock at the door; there is a call from France. Knut, his father. I walk over to the main house. The sun is shining, birds are singing, people are working in and around the guest house. A new day has started. The first day without him.

"Hello, Knut," tears once more.

Words are inadequate. How is it for a father to lose his son? I hear the pain in his voice, but he sounds calm and I am touched by the feeling coming through his words. However there are practical matters to discuss as well. Knut has involved the Norwegian consul in Jamaica and the necessary dignitaries in Norway, who can occupy themselves with the transport of the body. I'll talk from here with the consul. He will contact me again later in the day.

As soon as I come back to my room, I am called again; it's a call from Holland, from my mother. Now I can be the child for a moment and cry again. How close we are, there is no distance.

On my way back to my room, the cleaning women stare at me. They make weeping sounds. An American lady comes to express her sympathy and offers me her help. She helps me pack his backpack, that is all I can think of. When it is finished, we embrace. Anonymous humanity. It helps.

Everything has been packed now. I take his hand luggage with all his valuables with me. Carefully I pack his walkman, with the tape with his travel journal, which he recorded, the shell and the coral he picked up yesterday. The rest goes into the big backpack to travel with his body. I pick out some clothes for him, so they can dress him when he is to be placed on a bier. I choose his black trousers and white shirt. He may leave here well dressed. Just in case I even take black socks and shoes with me.

My own hand luggage is ready too. At last I carefully pack the small mother-of -pearl shell in my shoulder bag.

It is time to go to the police station.

John is ready by now too. He has not slept either . We get in his car and set off. The police station is only a ten minute drive. As soon as we arrive we are addressed by a police officer. We have to follow him back to the place of the accident, for a reconstruction. That is a disappointment, I had hoped to be able to go to him at once.

We drive back to the guest house and park at the side of the road. The sun is burning hot, cars are racing by. People are walking along the side of the road, on their way to their work, tourists going to the beach. Life continues as if nothing has happened. But a little further is a dried spot of blood as a silent witness. Nobody pays any attention to it.

There are two police cars driving with us and a mini bus, in which they have a man in handcuffs. Two policemen are pushing him forwards.

"That's the driver," John says.

What! Right after the accident I was so entirely caught up by Hermod, that I did not take any notice of anything else. Last night, when I was lying on the bed, it suddenly occurred to me that there must have been a driver in this car. I wondered whether this man had stopped, or driven on, and how he would have felt, how he would feel now.

According to John he had stopped after the accident and had been standing among the crowd around me. He was taken by the police and had spent the night in jail.

I walk towards him. He looks like an ordinary Jamaican. A dark man with rasta hair and a meek appearance, however now he is very shaken. When he sees me he clearly gets a fright and lowers his eyes. I stand in front of him and look at him straight. His brown eyes look beaten and afraid. He is as much a victim as I am, I realize. He must have driven like crazy, but they all do here. This is not a criminal, but they treat him like that. I do not feel anger, only compassion. For a moment I lay my hand on his shoulder.

"It has happened," I say, "You can't do anything about it any more either. Don't be afraid."

He does not respond and is brutally taken away. I feel rage coming up and pat the policeman on his shoulder.

"Can't you deal with this man in a normal way? He's not a criminal."

No reaction. Another policeman tells me to go with them as well. His tone does not appeal to me, but I do as I'm told. We walk along the dusty side of the road to the dried spot of blood.

You were lying here, my love. With chalk a rectangle has been drawn around it. I watch the cars racing by. Even in daytime they drive at breakneck speed. I could just walk under a car, then I can be with you....

They interrogate the driver, make busy gestures pointing towards the place where we crossed the road and the place where he fell on the road. There are some spectators standing around. A woman steps forward and screams to the policemen:

"It was an accident! I know this man, he is not a criminal, he would never harm a fly."

The policemen do not show any reaction. Two of them take notes from what the driver tells them. Two others measure the distance between the place where we crossed and the spot of blood. Until now they have ignored me completely. My irritation grows and I turn round and walk back to John.

"I think we can go."

But no, that seems not to be the case. One of the policemen who stayed with the cars tells me to stay. After what seems a long time of inefficient talking, writing and walking back and forth, they come to me. Now I have to show where we crossed, how we crossed, where exactly he was hit on the road. I experience everything over again. They ask me to estimate how fast the car was driving, but I refuse, I am not able to. In Holland one drives 50 km/hr in a built-up area. Here the rules are either different, or they are not obeyed. On this road one drives at 60 to 80 km/hr, at night even more. This man must have been driving extremely fast. Under normal speed, Hermod would, at the moment we noticed the car, easily have been able to cross in front of the car. We check everything exactly. They measure once more; it turns out that he was dragged by the car for about 30 metres.

It is getting too much for me, I want to get away from here, go to him. I want to see him again, physically.

Finally we are going back to the station. It is a drab concrete building. Inside we have to wait, then we are referred to a sergeant. In a small office, which hardly fits two chairs and a desk, we are received by a friendly sergeant, who looks at me sympathetically. He offers me his condolences, a chair for John and me and then he starts asking me questions.

On his desk are Hermod's passport and ticket. Apart from talking about details of the accident we discuss the identification I need to do at the mortuary and the transport of the body to Norway. We are interrupted several times by officers who enter the room and the sergeant is called away a few times. Nevertheless I have the feeling that for the first time since my contact with the local police, I am being heard, that something is happening.

He calls the local doctor. It turns out there has not been a physician with him yet, but he will come in the course of the day. I call the consul. It will not be possible to get his body on the same plane with me to London. We come to an agreement that his body will be on the plane tomorrow, if I can do the identification today. If we cannot meet the physician today, John could do the identification tomorrow, but I do not want that. I want to stay responsible.

A bit relieved we leave the sergeant's cramped office. Now to Hermod! No, we are being told to wait, I have to be interrogated once more. After a while I am led into a small dusty office, where there are two noisy police officers. Without even blinking at me they start to ask me questions about the accident in a very brutal way. This is the fourth time I have had to tell my story to the police. This time everything I say is slowly and meticulously written down, in their words, which they read out to me and I have to say whether I agree or not. Now and then I cannot follow their biting questions in their strong Jamaican accent.

"Don't you speak English?" they snap at me.

Meanwhile we are repeatedly interrupted. Several times they do not listen at all to my answers to their questions and I have to repeat myself again and again. Above my head they flirt with a cleaning woman who enters the room. I feel outraged and exhausted. I cannot control my rage and tears and impatience anymore. Never before have I been treated so brutally.

"When you ask me questions, I want you to listen to me!" I say and stand up and want to walk away.

They become angry too.

John comes in between:

"Elleke, I know it's difficult, but try to see it as a lesson in patience. They need to do their job and you have to cooperate, otherwise you won't be able to leave. You have to go through this. Please, hold on for a little while."

He is right. Hopelessly I sit down again.

Finally we are finished, I sign their report

The mortuary is 45 minutes away, driving inland. Silently I sit next to John and look outside. Behind the houses spread around are the fields under the palm trees. On the background blue hills. The country is as paradisical as ever. The events of the past night have not changed this. There are also signs of poverty, shabby huts, ravaged buildings and farmers tending one cow. Oh, Jamaica, how beautiful you are, but what a lot needs to happen to improve the welfare of your people.

I share my thoughts with John. He emphasises how his country lies far behind in development, in so many aspects. The total inefficiency at the police station is a good example. I agree with him, but I point out the beauty, the musicality and the relaxation in his country compared with the stress in western society.

I am still able to think of other things, I surprise myself.

We arrive at a village. There is the mortuary, another tasteless concrete building. With a sick feeling in my stomach I go inside. We are received by the employees with a professional mixture of appropriate respect and indifference. The physician has not arrived yet and noone knows whether he will come today, so no identification can take place now, but I am allowed to see Hermod's body. Someone points to the next room. I go inside. It is cool and there is a smell of death. There are several figures under white clothes. He lies next to a small figure. Like the Christ child folded in clothes, his face, a part of his breast and an arm are lying free and his feet stick out. It is him and it is not him. It is so obvious that he is not in this body any more. But it is the covering in which I have known him and which I have loved. Here it lies like a wax sculpture. I look at his face with his beautiful features, his pronounced cheekbones and jaws, his mouth, which could be closed so headstrongly, so vulnerable when he was asleep, so determined when he kissed me. I stroke his hair and lay my hand on his breast and am flooded by a wave of love and sadness.

" Don't touch him!" they scream behind me.

They can all go to hell. I remain as I stand. After taking in his whole image I let go of him.

An indescribable emptiness.

We leave his backpack behind, labelled and with a description of the contents together with the clothes I have chosen for him.

Outside I am addressed by a woman, who asks whether he was my husband and she expresses her sympathy. She turns out to be the mother of the small child figure which was lying next to him. The child had been severely ill and handicapped since the birth. There are other people suffering too... I express my sympathy with her.

We drive back. It is afternoon by now. I am so exhausted that I lie down on the seat in the back of the car. I need to disappear for a while, to flee into sleep. Which drops over me like a black blanket.

When I wake up we are back at the police station. John addresses the sergeant once more to urge the physician to come to the mortuary this afternoon in order to do the identification. He succeeds. We have an appointment at three o'clock. Then we go to the bank. I still need to get money to pay John. He says that money is not important right now, but I think he does not need to be bothered because we were late with the payment of our last nights. Beside the bank is the shop with T-shirts.

"It may seem crazy and totally irrelevant now, but in this shop I've had a T-shirt reserved for Yoram, my son. I'll fetch it anyway, it's important to him to get something as well. His sisters will each get a dress."

John waits patiently outside. He is fantastic.

Actually I wanted to buy T-shirts for Hermod's nephews as well, as he intended to do so today, but I cannot sort it all out now. I am only capable of doing things that can be done on autopilot.

We drive back to the guest house. There are a lot of phone messages waiting: Anja, my sister, who offers to go with me to Norway. I am grateful for that. I cannot have better support than hers. Then Cecilie calls, his other sister. We cry together and I feel I am not alone in my sorrow, even though I am alone here in Jamaica in this disaster, I am not standing alone. In between the phone calls I try to rest a bit on the bed, but there is little opportunity. As soon as I lie down for a moment and relax, I feel him, he is still there. I feel consoled.

There is a knock again. Knut calls to ask how things have been going and to discuss the transport. I agree that the Norwegian consulate will inform the airline and reserve a seat for me, because I will be late getting to the airport, later than is normally accepted for check-in to international flights, because I need to do the identification. I ask them to reserve an empty seat next to me out of respect for him. I would not be able to stand sitting next to someone else right now.

Pearl, John's mother, has a pan of soup ready for us. John sits down to eat, but my stomach has a knot inside. I refuse politely and after her insisting I accept a banana. The banana does me good. I realize the lobster salad of yesterday afternoon has been digested by now. I am glad I enjoyed that salad, that he let me enjoy that salad. Those few extra dollars it cost seem so totally irrelevant now.

I still have to go to the diving school to bring back his book and to say that he will not come for his final exam. When I come to the road and have to cross where we crossed yesterday evening, I intend not to look to the right or left. Anybody can knock me down. But nothing happens. I pass the spot of blood. Nobody has taken the effort to wash it away. It has faded a bit, by the passing traffic. A dark brown spot. It won't be visible any more after a couple of days.

At the diving school the girls are sitting on the veranda. They look up when I approach. I do not know how to start, but they read from my face that there is something. Bluntly I blurt out that he will not be coming for his test because he had an accident yesterday evening here on the street and I start to cry.

Of course they get a tremendous shock and put their arms around me and ask what they can do for me. There is nothing to be done. Yesterday he was still here, radiant and dancing with the movement of the breath in the neutral buoyancy.

Sven is devastated too. After sitting together for a while, I ask whether I can get my diving certificate. It seems almost inappropriate, but what else can I do? He writes it out with tears in his eyes.

Then I say goodbye and walk to the beach. I take off my slippers. The sand feels hot on my bare feet. Reggae music sounds in my ears. People are having their holidays as if life just goes on.

I walk into the sea and step around in the shallow water. The spurting water drops look like silver pearls. Farewell ocean, I would love to dive into you, to wash everything off, to drown myself in you. I never want to leave you. But life does seem to continue and now I have to go to the mortuary and next to go home, to my children and to Norway, to give him a beautiful funeral.

Afterwards we shall see. Farewell, I do not know whether I

shall ever come back here, but I shall see you in every sea I swim in, at every beach I shall walk on. All seas and oceans are one.

Walking back to the guest house I pass a small shop. Then it occurs to me that I can buy some small presents for his nephews with my last Jamaican dollars, colourful purses, which I had also bought for my children and two decorated pencils for the little ones. This I can decide on autopilot.

"I hope you agree with these choices, dear. Otherwise you shouldn't have postponed it until the end. Now at least they have something, indirectly from you."

It seems as if he smiles.

When I reach the guest house it is time to leave.

I say goodbye to the family and to the cleaning women, leaving the rest of the Jamaican dollars on the table.

"You are a strong woman, stay strong," Pearl says when she flings her round arms around me.

"How can you say so, when I'm walking around crying all the time."

"You may be crying, but I feel you have a big strength. Keep using it!"

I feel what she means, my sorrow is my sorrow, but underneath I feel my core, my self.

Pearl has insisted that John has us driven by a friend of his, because he is also exhausted after last night. It would be irresponsible to drive now. His friend has arrived and while John fetches something out of the house, I ask his friend to take good care of him for the next few days, he has had a big shock as well. The friend promises.

The taxi driver arrives, the one Hermod had arranged yesterday, properly on the time agreed. I am sorry for this man. John insists on bringing me himself, and I am grateful. Suddenly I realize that, had Hermod not changed our tickets yesterday, I would not have been able to leave on this flight. I would have been stuck here.

Silently we drive to the mortuary. The physician has arrived too and all I need to do is declare in his presence that this body belonged to Hermod. We enter the room. Again the smell of death. There he lies.

"Do you know this man?"

"Yes, this is my friend, my love."

This is being recorded in writing including all personal details.

The physician announces that he will do an autopsy and disappears into the other room leaving the doors open. An autopsy? The man who finishes the paperwork with me explains that this is because it was an accident and the case will come to court. The very thought that people will cut into his body with professional indifference is unbearable to me and who knows what else they will do. I need to be there, watching, so it is done respectfully. I walk in.

"I want to see everything and I want you to tell me exactly what you're doing and why you're doing it."

The physician looks at me straight. He explains that he has to determine the most direct cause of death. Therefore they need to investigate him internally. I take position at the side and watch how two assistants in white coats start off.

I cannot go deeper to the bottom, I realize. It cannot get worse. If I had not yet fully realized he is dead, I realize now. And yet it is not as horrifying as the moment of the accident and the first minutes I saw him lying in the street. I watch with a mixture of devastation and love. This is not him, this is only his body. But I have loved his body too and I still love it. I know him inside and outside. Now I see inside his body. I see his heart, his lungs... The physician explains and shows how both his heart and his lungs have been ruptured. I see it with my own eyes.

He must have been killed instantly. No soul could have returned to this damaged body.

I feel - see - him standing beside me. For a moment he lays his hand on my shoulder, then takes my hand. I feel his love. Hand in hand we watch his body being analysed. This is absurd, I think. This is an absurd situation.

I do not perceive any fear or pain in him. He watches with amazement and resignation, love and a sort of knowing. I only feel bewilderment and love, no resignation and I do not know anything. I am not able to communicate with him, at least not in words, but we know that we feel each other. We feel what is going on inside each other.

John has entered the room. Silently and seriously he watches. Two policemen have entered as well. I notice they keep an eye on me to see whether I can cope. I think this quite considerate. So far I have not had that much consideration from the police officers here. They do not notice Hermod standing here beside me.

The physician examines his eyes and lifts an eyelid. I look at it. It is his eye, but he does not look through it any more. Eyes are the gateways of the soul. These gateways are empty.

When they want to establish how much brain damage there is, I walk outside. There are limits to my capacity. Two minutes later I come back. I want to see with my own eyes how they restore what they have caused. It is hard to believe that he can still be shown to the family properly in state. But they promise me and they will succeed. I take a last glance at his body... see you soon in Norway.

In the office I check whether everything is in order, the papers, his luggage. When everything is all right, he will be flown over tomorrow.

In the car on the way to the airport I want to disappear again, away from everything. It is as if he puts his arm around me. I fall into some kind of comatose sleep and do not wake up until hours later, when we arrive at the airport. John helps me, literally he puts me and my luggage in front of the right check-in desk. Once more he gives me a card with his address. In the course of the night and the day I have thanked him several times for everything he has done for me. Now I am out of words, and I say this to him. We embrace.

"Goodbye my friend. I'll never forget what you have done for me."

"Stay strong."

Without looking back he walks away.

I know he is moved.

I check in and walk through the departure hall with my and his shoulderbag over my shoulders. Another 20 minutes before departure. Seldom have I felt so lost. First I go to the toilet, refresh myself and put on my bodysuit and tights. Next I stroll along some shops. Out of most of the shops Bob Marley sounds towards me. It makes me feel even more lonely. In front of my eyes I see his radiant, sweaty face when we danced... I feel empty and feeble and buy a mug with mangojuice and a few tamarind balls. At a jewelry shop I stand still and look at the pearl jewels.

The pearl, I have found it, within myself and within our love. You have found it too, it is our pearl.

The lady of the shop looks at me in a friendly way:

"Are you going back home? Have you enjoyed your holidays?"

I do not know what to say.

"Don't mention it."

"Was it so wonderful or so terrible?"

I cannot keep it to myself.

"Well, since you ask me. We had a most wonderful time, but yesterday evening, our last evening, my boyfriend had an accident."

"Oh, is that you. I just heard in the news. I'm so terribly sorry for you! I wish you a lot of strength."

"Thank you. I need to go now. My plane is leaving."

In the plane I nestle myself into the seat reserved for me next to the window. The seat beside me is empty. I feel bewildered and numbed. I look out of the window. It is getting dark outside. The images I now see of the country will be the last. Farewell, Jamaica. I do not know whether I shall ever come back.

It is only a short hop to Kingston, 20 minutes, to take off and to land. The safety belts stay on. We have a short stop in Kingston. A sympathic man comes to sit on the other side of Hermod's empty seat. We introduce ourselves. His name is Hugh and he comes from Ireland. When he makes an attempt to store his luggage, I tell him that he can use the empty seat as well, because it will stay empty. He looks surprised, for the plane is streaming full around us. When I say I have reserved the empty seat he looks even more surprised. I want to tell him. We shall fly for hours and when I need to cry, it is better if he knows what is wrong.

"I was with my boyfriend, he had an accident yesterday evening."

How terrible it sounds, I can't get used to it. How many times shall I have to tell this? Hugh reacts sympathetically in a pleasant, reserved way. We talk a little. I feel it is okay with him if I do not want to speak. And I do not want to right now. I want to rest, to disappear, to sleep. Tears are welling up. I close my eyes, pull a blanket around me and fold my legs on the empty chair. I feel you around me. It even seems a bit like on our way to Jamaica, how I fell asleep on your lap, in your arms.

I feel you are free and are trying to convince me that death is not a disaster.

"It doesn't end with death. Our reality, life on earth within duality, is limited. Open yourself to a wider reality. There is only reality."

I hear this in words, but I feel you are saying much more than this. This communication goes beyond words.

My reality is limited now, I know that. You have space. 'Breathe in and up we go, breathe out and down we go.'

And here I am with my pain, my sorrow and my broken dreams. And what about all my beautiful premonitions? What about my trust in the future? It was a possibility. I believed in it and you had started to believe in it as well, but destiny has decided otherwise. I cannot accept it. What has happened is what I have always feared. But recently I had let go of my fear, trusting that I would not lose you anymore.

I do not begrudge you your peace at all, my love, but I do not know how to live on without you. Life seemed so much to open itself to us. There seemed such potential for growth together. I still see your eyes radiating, when you talked about the timelessness which is there between us. And yet it does seem as if our relationship continues in another reality, as you say. But I want to be there too, I do not want to be here any more. I have always been so eager for life, for happiness. Now I do not feel this longing any more. I have been very happy in my life and most of all together with you.

With you, all my wishes have come true. You have been a most precious gift.You, with your brightness, intelligence, sincerity, creativity, humour, and infinite tenderness, but also with your strongheadedness, stubbornness, fearfulness and anger. You have given and taught me such a lot, inspired me and made me aware of the opposites, the paradoxes of life. Thanks to you I have opened up, started to flourish, become more alert. Together we experienced an inflow of inspiration and talked about the importance of the outflow of creativity. But now how to continue?

When I think of the children I feel love, as well as for the people around me. I am longing to be with them. At least that is a beginning. I am longing to write - to write everything down, to give expression to our love, our inspiration, my love, my pain. That is another longing. And will I be able to continue working with my clients? Maybe, after some time. Will I be able to teach again? I hope I shall feel up to it. The management consultancy? No idea. The job in London? No idea. Taking care of the children? Yes!

The only thing I can do is try to stay with the pearl. If I have to continue my life, I want to live in freedom, in love. I will not force myself to do anything any more. I do not have to work, I will allow myself to do what I like, according to what lives in my heart. With you all my fears and insecurities have died. The time with you has been a major lesson in love. You have given me the experience of complete surrender to love. And we have not reached the limits of it yet. Probably there are no limits to it.

We were growing so much, could have continued to grow for a whole lifetime!

"It has been a touch, an experience, a timeless dolphin meeting, healing for both of us."

Suddenly I feel – is it through you? – a glimpse of insight that this event may create space for something else, something of inexplicable beauty, which is not to be overseen by me yet. It is a lesson in letting go. The glimpse of insight disappears immediately. Please, stay in touch, teach me. You are the one who is beyond now.

Maybe I should not ask myself too much and scream - like you always did - why, why, why? I do not want this at all. I do not want to be here.

But I do scream, for apart from some flashes of insight and waves of love and gratitude, I am also feeling furious, helpless and incredibly sad.

The flight goes quickly. I let myself be disturbed as little as possible by the stewardesses with their meals and snacks. I am hungry, though I have little appetite. I withdraw into my cocoon and sleep, doze and cry inwardly.

When we approach London I feel literally and metaphorically approaching the earth. 'Ordinary' reality is coming closer. Here in London we would have had a few hours to say goodbye and to relish the memory of the journey. See you next month, we would have said.

Crying I pass through customs. They ask what is wrong. Hugh, who is standing behind me, explains and puts his arm around me.

"Is there someone to pick you up?"

"Yes, in Holland they are waiting for me and here I'll go to friends. I'll be okay. Thank you for now."

We say goodbye.

In the central hall of the airport I find a phone box. I want to call Stephen and Linda. This journey started with them, now I want to share everything with them. And they need to know anyway. Happily they are at home. When I hear their voices, I realize once more that we had really become friends during that evening, because they are Hermod's friends, but mainly because it clicks at soul level. Time turns out to be too short to see each other - London is bigger than I think - but we have a long and good talk. Stephen says they were delighted to see us together. They saw this was love, the love Hermod had always longed for. He is convinced Hermod and I have helped each other to transcend to another level of being and that our relationship continues.

I can honour our love in my relationship with the children, with the people around me, maybe one day in a new relationship. I can see this is true. Stephen makes me aware of something else. Despite his fear of commitment, of this commitment which was extra complicated with the three children involved, he had gone for it, he had embraced all four of us.

Squatting on the floor beside the phone box I reflect on the talk. The last bit is true as well. You gave all you had to give and that is an incredible amount. Every minute with you was worth it. All the struggles we went through have been enriching and each time we came out of it we were better off than before. Compared with the pearl the struggles were peanuts.

"Jeg elsker deg i tidløshet." "I love you in timelessness."

I know your family and friends have received from your gifts as well. That has become very clear to me in all the phone talks of the last two days. So actually I should say: "Vi er glad i deg i tidløshet." "We love you in timelessness."

It is just that I had wanted so much to continue with you, at least for 40 years.

Gradually I begin to see how we can continue together, while you are there and I am here, in the timeless realm. I wish I could feel, hear and see you even more clearly. Maybe I can learn this.

"We have to learn to communicate through the atmospheres," you once said at a goodbye at Oslo airport. We were able to, whether we were physically together or not, often we were wirelessly connected. I still feel this. You also said:

"Maybe it's possible to live in different realities at the same time, since time is not linear anyway."

We often talked about this. Now you are encouraging me to open myself to this. Yet I doubt: What is real? It is my reality, I can make of it whatever is meaningful to me. There is one thing I am certain about: our love is real and exists beyond time and space. Now I know I can never lose you. I lost my fears instead. Nor am I afraid anymore of failure in anything, for, like you said:"... and so what?"

My legs are getting stiff from being folded for such a long time. The talk and my own reflections have done me good. As if I have gained some strength. There is another half an hour before my plane leaves. I have found five English pounds in his wallet. I shall give myself a treat. He would probably approve of that. I buy a bottle of perfume oil with a scent of ocean and a bar of chocolate with the last pennies. Then I become fascinated by a book in a shop and finally I have to run on my way to the gate. Tap, tap, tap, tap, my heels go in a hurry. For an instant I experience déjà vu.

Once in the plane I reflect on what is lying ahead. Now the last little piece of a long journey is coming and altogether I feel better than when I left Jamaica on my way back home. By resting I have been able to take the first step of digesting a bit.

I am not looking forward to my arrival, though I am looking

forward to seeing the children, but everything will be painful. I have asked Peter to prepare them a bit for the fact that I am feeling sad and possibly I shall cry now and then.

Peter, Anja, her boyfriend Andy and my mother will be there. Then there will be a lot to be arranged at home; appointments for the next week will have to be cancelled and I want to fly to Norway as soon as possible.

First resting a bit.

I close my eyes and before I know we are landing at Schiphol.

4

Time

I can't stand it
Every second, hour, day
takes me further away from you
You've become history
in our time

Yet you're part of me
living through me
in the present
As well as I'm part of you
dying through you
in the present
In transcendence
we meet beyond
in timelessness
the eternal
now

Schiphol, March

I wash my face in the bathroom and rub some cream onto my skin, which has become dry from all the salty tears. I watch myself in the mirror. Unrealistically my mirror self stares back. Apart from my eyes, which look stern, I am looking well, healthy, tanned, and strangely enough, strong. That's just as well, I shall need all my strength for the coming period.

I fetch my luggage, take a deep breath and walk through the gate.

There they are.

Tara jumps at me, Imre follows behind her. Their faces are

pale, with red cheeks and bright eyes. How beautiful they are, how lovely, and how it hurts now to feel love. I bend and put my arms around them. Do not cry right now, do not cry! Yoram comes to me, open, disciplined, sweet. Behind them stand Peter, my mother, Anja and Andy. We embrace.

The first thing Yoram says is: "Elleke, I wish you'd taken my drawing for Hermod with you, then at least he'd have seen it."

His eyes are shining with tears.

"Now I want you to take it with you to Norway and lie it on his coffin..."

I say this is okay, I tell him I had told him about the drawing and that he was looking forward to seeing it in April.

My arms are filled with children, a small hand here, a kiss there.

I feel we belong together, but it is as if I have come from another planet. I am a different woman from the one who left for Jamaica. They do not know this. We walk to the cars and drive home.

At home everything looks as I once left it. There are flowers, it is clean and made cosy with care. The furniture, the floor, the children's toys, everything is as it was before. Only I have changed.

The children want to tell me everything at once, what they have been going through, these past three weeks. I try to listen attentively, but now and then I cannot follow. It trumpets in my ears. They have had a good time, this much is clear to me, up until the last two days, when they heard about the accident. Yoram has had a headache for two days and Tara has cried a lot. Only Imre has been quite joyful. Why, she explains herself:

"Hermand has become an angel, so now he can always be with us."

That is a reason for joy indeed, though I cannot feel the joy.

After dinner we sit together with tea and coffee and proudly the children go around with Easter eggs. Easter eggs! Symbol of new life. Spring has started and it is almost Easter.... Then Imre knocks herself and comes to me for comfort. When I feel her round little body shaking in my arms, something breaks inside. Together we cry. She looks at me, my crying makes her stop. She is not shocked, lovingly she wipes the tears from my face. For a long time we sit together, my body folded around hers in my lap. Silently the others sit around. I tell the children a little bit of what happened. A few pieces, they are not open for more right now, which is fine with me. I put them to bed. Yoram and Tara are crying:

"I wish he had become our father. I love him. I don't want him to be dead!"

I cry with them and tell them life does not end with death. He is still there, but not in the form we know him. But he loves us, me and them, this I am certain about.

Now the children are in bed, we can talk a bit more. I tell some bits and pieces.

Knut rings. We discuss the cremation and the announcement in the newspaper. I appreciate the way they involve me in all this.

My mother and Andy go home. Peter will stay nearby until I am back from Norway in order to help. Anja stays overnight.

Exhausted I fall on my bed, but I cannot sleep. I feel empty and torn apart.

Two messy days follow: these are week days.The children have to go to school. Life seems to continue as normal. Peter takes care of this. Anja goes home to prepare to go to Norway with me. I book a flight, call back and forth with the family in Norway about the funeral.

In Jamaica problems arise about the transportation of his body. They are unclear about who will finance this. This will be his insurance, but this information seems not to get through.

I call John to say I have arrived safely. I cancel my clients and students for the next two weeks and ask them to call me back eventually to make a new appointment. I do not know what I will feel up to at that time. I may want rest for half a year to re-orientate my life. People react very understandingly and sympathetically. Friends and family call. A packet arrives from London, with a card from Stephen and Linda and the alarm clock he had bought for us and we had forgotten in London. Vidar, his best friend calls. There is a lot to talk about. We shall do this as soons as I arrive in Norway. Neighbours and friends come by to express their sympathy. Cards drop in the mailbox and flowers are being delivered. I feel supported from all sides. It makes the pain a little more bearable, but does not lessen it.

I unpack my bag, wash my sarongs and summer clothes and pack my dark winter clothes and gloves – it is freezing in Norway – and my black dress, which he liked so much and my black silk jacket.

I do everything in a daze, but at the same time I feel clear as crystal. Crystal clear and unreal. It is as if I have no skin. I feel naked and vulnerable. All impressions come in amplified. Meanwhile I cry.

When the children come home, I want to be there for them, but the phone keeps on ringing and I am absorbed by everything.

The pictures have been developed. They are beautiful and they reflect our happiness. There are a few pictures for Imre, of his efforts with the sand-seahorses and of a pig with piglets, coming out of the bushes on one of our trips. Quickly he had taken two pictures:

"For Imre!" he had said triumphantly.

She likes them.

I also listen to the tape with his recorded holiday diary. His warm voice sounds deep and relaxed. Accurately and with joy he describes paradise...

In all this hectic business there is no time to digest, or to be with him with my attention. Only in the evening, when I withdraw to my work room, there is a moment of rest. I unpack my hand luggage. My small shell, his big shell and the piece of coral I lay on my desk, together with the stone box, in the shape of a graceful shell, the first present he gave me.

"To me this symbolises Elleke," he said at that time.

After his departure I found a wooden nut inside.

"Did you find the nut?" he asked over the phone, when he was back home.

"That is my life, my essence in a nutshell, which I leave with you."

I sink into silence. I feel him, I feel the love, connecting us as souls. But on the personality level I feel pain, pain, pain. My big love gone, my future.

And why? I feel he is free, where he always longed to be. But what about me?

I hardly sleep for two nights. The exhaustion makes me feel even more shaky.

Then it is time to leave again. With difficulty I say goodbye to the children. It is too much to have to leave them behind once more. It's too much for them as well. I would rather take them with me, they want to come, but I cannot make it. I need all my energy to be there, with his family and friends, preparing for the funeral. All the conversations will be in English and Norwegian. They would hardly be able to participate. On Saturday early in the morning Andy takes Anja and me to Schiphol airport. Had it not been for the reason for this trip, we would have enjoyed flying together. Last time we travelled together was almost two years ago, in Australia, on the dolphin research. Now and then we can have fun for an instant, but immediately a cloud of tears floats by.

When we fly over the familiar, snow-covered landscape, with the hills and pine trees, it cuts through me. Hermod's country, the country I have grown to love, which I thought would become my home...

Norway is not the same Norway any more.

Oslo, March

At Gardemoen, the airport, Jan-Marcus and Beate are waiting for us. They have been as tense about this meeting as we have. All of us are a bit afraid of the pain of the confrontation. But it is all right. Tears and love.

I thank them for the warm way I have been received by the whole family.

It is good at Knut's place as well, where we come together with Cathrine. I am aware how much I love this family and I feel their affection reaching out to me. We cry, share, talk, and bring back memories. I show them some pictures and tell them about our last weeks. Knut calls Jamaica. It is still unclear when the body will be transported. The funeral has to be postponed.

Then Anja and I go to his apartment. With trembling hands I open the door. It is home, it is his. It is very familiar, it is empty. I cry with long shrieking howls. I'm grateful that Anja is with me.

I walk around and greet all the familiar belongings. His furniture, his books, his personal things like the aeolian harp, bought in Amsterdam, tinkling softly. The two small shell-shaped stone boxes, belonging with the box I got from him. Pictures of me are spread out all over the place.

In the bedroom I find the eleven troll children, that I made for him as a surprise for St. Nicholas. Once he said there were eleven troll children living in his heart, who sometimes turn into a dragon. I made the trolls and wrote a poem about troll children, hiding from the light, being invited with love to dance and play, so they would be able to find the most precious gift; which they did.

There are flowers, with a card attached from the nephews. And the apartment has been tidied up. Cathrine and Jan-Marcus have been here to clear up. He had left it in chaos. I would rather have come in to his chaos, I know him and I love him, including his rubbish. But I appreciate their effort and care.

We find two boxes with chocolate-marzipan hearts. In the kitchen I find a small pot of mouldy pesto, which I had bought at Christmas for a dinner we had with his friends. I had warned him that pesto cannot be kept for long. A bachelor's household!

We light some candles, make tea and play some soft harp music. It is good to be here, it is home. There is no place I would rather be right now than here, in his atmosphere.

Silently we sit on the couch and take everything in. A peace is descending. For the first time since the accident I do not have to do anything. He is very close.

Then the harp music slowly fades away and we hear a rhythmic, penetrating bumping of a heartbeat. We look at each other. A low voice starts to sing:

'I'm breathing in life, I'm breathing in her...I'm breathing in the darkness of love and total joy. It's beautiful here, with you!...'

I am gasping for breath. It is almost too weird. He must have listened to this CD before he left. He has a CD player which can contain several CDs and play them automatically in sequence. The music continues:

'I decide for the world, I decide to be born. But what shall I think of world, what shall I do in this world?...'

Yes, I think, finally you have chosen life... and you have been taken away.

We sleep in his bed. I got some light sleeping pills from Jan Marcus. The whole family is using them at the moment. We need our energy to get through the days. I have never used any sleeping tablets before. I take a half and for the first time since the accident I fall into a deep sleep. When I wake up and cry, Anja is there.

In the morning, after a shower, I sit down in silence. Just like the night of the accident I feel him inside and around me, closer than ever. He is beyond now and beyond his earthly limitations. I feel his freedom, his radiance... and a dash of sadness and a desperate longing to be with me, or is it my own longing? I hesitate. What is real?

He is standing in front of me, smiles and strokes my face, my shoulder, my arm. I feel his longing, his touch, almost physically. My body reacts with a shiver.

"I'm there! We are together, here, now! Trust your perception and be with me."

"I do, deep inside, but there is doubt as well."

"Trust, please."

I decide to trust and try to open myself to him. I struggle to be able to touch him, to be with him. It is as if my consciousness expands, as if I rise somehow. We touch in timelesness...

With a shock I am back. I feel strengthened and consoled. Real or not is of no relevance. This experience is authentic, real for me. It is totally different from when I think of him, or when I imagine him as he was.

The way I experience him is not entirely new to me. When my father died when I was eighteen, I also had some contact with him and to some extent we were able to communicate. During the pregnancies of the children I had similar experiences when I was able to communicate with them. Those experiences were less intense than what is happening now. This is different. Hermod and I have a different relationship, we are a unit, like he said.

We spend the morning at home, talking, pondering, reading. On his desk I find a book by Thich Nhat Hanh, a buddhistic teacher, by whom he was very inspired 'Be still and know' * it is called. It is full of beautiful reflections, like:

'Reality is quite different from our concepts.'

There you are, I think. I can let go of all my concepts and open myself to my experiences. And also:

'The greatest relief is to touch the ultimate dimension of reality. Once you are capable of touching the ocean's water, you will not be afraid of

the being and nonbeing as well as the coming and going of the waves.'

This has been our quest, and it still is. But I am not afraid any more of the coming and going of the waves. All my fears have died together with him.

'If, when we practice, we are not aware that the world is suffering, that children are dying of hunger, that social injustice is going on a little bit everywhere, we are not practising mindfulness. We are just trying to escape.'

You were most aware of this and you wanted to contain the suffering of the world in mindfulness, but this fell heavily on you.

'The miracle is not to walk on water. The miracle is to walk on the green earth, dwelling deeply in the present moment and feeling truly alive.'

You knew all this. Why then did you leave?

There is another book by Thich Nhat Hanh, *The Sun My Heart*.* I open it right at a page with a wonderful text about the illusion of death and the continuity of life. I decide I shall read it out at the funeral ceremony. I find it difficult to nose around in his things. What does he want and what not? And yet... we were about to live together. I was allowed to know him, with all his sides. Probably he is okay with me being here. A present lies on his desk, wrapped in the same paper as the present I got from him for Christmas as a taste of what he had in store for me. Would this be my Christmas present? It should be. He said it was ready waiting for me and that the two presents belonged together. Hesitantly I open it. It is a small silk toilet bag, in beautiful sea blue-green colour, indeed belonging with the comb in the silk purse I had got earlier. I know the story behind these two presents. Thank you, love!

We go for a stroll. Through the snowy streets to Vigeland park, a huge park with impressive statues, representing the human cycle of existence. The first time I was here was with him and later I came here several times on my own. It is good to be outside. Besides Anja has not seen anything of Oslo yet. At the pedestrian crossing, there is a car approaching. I step back, Anja continues quietly. For an instant I get a shock, see a flash on my retina, but nothing happens. I realize I am traumatised. I had already noticed that I am more shocked by unexpected sounds than before. I tell her.

"Well, yes, you are traumatised," she states plainly. "This will take some time."

We spend the afternoon with the family again. Cecilie has come as well, with little Frederik, born on Hermod's last birthday and named after him. When I take this beautiful little being in my arms, tears well up again. Babies and small children evoke love and love hurts right now.

Besides it reminds me of the child we might have had together and possibly almost would have had by now. A few months ago I was overdue. He was shocked and happy.

"If this is the case, then life has chosen for me," he said. "There are all kinds of things running inside me, but one thing I feel very clearly: I have all faith in you and in our relationship, that we can accomplish this together."

When finally my period broke through, he said:

"Maybe this soul can come back to us later, when I am more ready."

I look at the little one in my arms. You were born on his birthday, but you are no replacement for him, you are you and you are fine and beautiful the way you are.

We talk, cry and share once more.

In the evening Christiane arrives, Knut's friend. Some time after Hermod's mother died, Knut met an old French friend from 40 years ago. This has developed into a flourishing relationship.

She has now come to support him.

At home I start calling Hermod's friends abroad. There are quite a few of them. I am on the phone for a long time, with people whom I mainly know from anecdotes, and they know me. Lines of connectedness are crossing over the planet. Some friends from Germany, Denmark and Sweden will come for the funeral. Vidar has called most of his Norwegian friends. After the phone calls I relax and sit down for a meditation.

I have hardly closed my eyes, and he is standing in front of me, radiant and well. He takes my hands.

"Come, up we go," he says.

With a sudden tug I am being pulled out of my body. Amazed I look down. My body is sitting there relaxed with crossed legs on the floor. I am standing in my appearance of light in front of him, my hands still in his hands. To make sure, I look down once more, my physical body is still sitting there immobile. I am here.

"Do you trust me?" he asks.

"Yes."

And he pulls me further on. We put our arms around each other and kiss. It feels so real and as good as in our most intimate embraces when he was still alive. Alive? He is still there! It is like when he still had a physical body.

After a timeless moment, we let go of each other. He looks at me earnestly:

"It wasn't my conscious decision to leave. If I had been able to come back, I would have come back, because of our love. But now I'll always be there for you, for to me there is no time and no space. It is effortless to be there for you."

For a moment I doubt myself, and him. Am I not imagining this? Immediately I fade away and almost fall. He prevents this by holding me.

"Stay! Trust!"

I try to open up again. I feel him again. I try to listen with my heart. A fragment of a sentence comes through:

"... healed my life."

"I had wished to heal you more."

"You are still healing me...."

"Uh?"

"By the way you are dealing with my passing, with my family, my friends, the way you are in my house.... the way you are with me: your love is healing for me. And I love you even more now I see how you are doing all this. I'm very grateful to you."

"You have healed me too and you are still healing me, with your love. You have been a major gift in my life. Life has given you to me and taken you away, yet you are still there..."

A thought comes to my mind, that actually, after a long prelude, we had only really been together for one and a half years... it feels as if it were a whole life, but it was so short... what can it mean to him, now he is in another reality? I feel a glimpse of uncertainty. Immediately I fall down. He holds me once more.

"Our love isn't less worthy, because it has been brief in earthly time. It is eternal. There is no time! We are together in timelessness."

"You are right. I know it, I feel it. But it is so hard to comprehend."

"... And you shouldn't be uncertain about the way you're in my house either. You're doing fine."

So he has felt this as well. Apparently there are no limits.

I become tired and cannot concentrate any more. Now I am indeed sinking. With a shock I am back in my body. I still feel him around, but I am not able to communicate with him anymore. I want to sleep.

At night I dream that he is angry and irritated and I am becoming insecure and want things to be okay between us, because I know he will die. I realize I am still carrying some uncertainties with me. Our relationship has been a human relationship, with human imperfections, although we had cosmic feelings now and then. I presumably need to give a place to those imperfections. It is good to be able to talk about all these things with Anja. She gives me support and feedback.

In my meditation the next day he is there again. I do not have to make any effort. He pulls me out of my body and we are together. He dances with me and swings me around. We are free and weightless, even more than in the sea. I feel he is longing for me as much as I am longing for him. He is glad I can be with him in this way.

"I have loved you more and love you more than I have been able to express in my life," he says solemnly.

I think of his words half a year ago, when he said, almost desperately: "Elleke, I love you more than I can tell you, there are no words for it! I wish I could shower you in love!"

"You have told me," I answer, as solemnly, " I have always felt your love, from the very beginning. You have showered me in love and now I can feel it even more clearly than ever."

I feel his essence and mine. This is real, I realize, this is more authentic than our personalities. This is who we truly are. His essence is not different from when he still had a body. It feels exactly the same. He is just more of his essence and more detached from his emotions and human limitations. This means that he can perceive me more clearly and I can perceive him.

When I cannot hold the energy any longer, he brings me back to my body, like bringing me home after a date. We say goodbye with an embrace, but it is not a goodbye.

"I stay with you, I am there, even when you are not aware of me."

"I feel your comfort and support, I feel you around me."

My brain turns around in my skull when I try to understand what is happening here. Every psychologist would think this is wishful thinking. But inside I knów. The experience is too authentic to question. If I can accept this as a reality, it is only healing.

I meditate every morning and evening and I do not have to make an effort at any time. He is there and he takes me with him.

In the afternoon we have an appointment with the whole

family at the university, with a professor who is also a priest and who will conduct the ceremony. Together we sketch an image of Hermod. It is an emotional event for all of us and we know we are being supported by each other, yet each of us is dealing with our sorrow in our own way. We are each of us in a different process and we can respect this in each other. Little Frederik goes from hand to hand as a comfort.

The next day flowers have been delivered, from his friends, to support me. Anja goes into town to explore a bit on her own.

Vidar will come today. I take the card, which Hermod wrote to Vidar the last but one day, but had not posted. It is written in Norwegian:

'Dear Vidar,

Now Elleke and I are sitting in a beach café and looking out over the golden sand and the emerald green water (like the picture on the card) of the sea, which turns more blue and blue until she meets the sky on the horizon. We are waiting for our lunch, after having our first scuba dive session this morning.

We've had a good time and we're having a good time!

I can tell you more about this paradise-like experience when I'm back.

*Hope you**

Hermod

There is also a tiny wooden painted match box, which he had bought for Vidar. Later he regretted this, for he did not want to give anything that would encourage his smoking. But I decide to give it to him anyway and to add this story. Matches serve to light candles and to bring light too.

There he comes, a tall, warm man. We have not met often before. When I was in Norway, Hermod and I had the inclination to spend all the time we had together. I think we cancelled three appointments with Vidar. It does not matter. We are close, knowing he shared so much with both of us. He shared other things with him, about me.

Vidar says that from the beginning he had the feeling I was the right woman for Hermod. Hermod had this feeling too, he said we have the same soul. This touches me, this is how it feels to me.

But, as with everything, he hesitated. Especially, because he found it so complicated that there were three children involved. Vidar knows everything in detail about Yoram, Tara and Imre. Hermod experienced them as if they were his own children, but felt guilty towards Peter about this.

When we contemplated going to Jamaica, he hesitated a lot. He and Vidar spent a whole afternoon in a café talking about it. He said that if he took me away from my children once more, he would go all the way and choose for our family, a choice for a lifetime. He never told me this so explicitly, that the decision to go to Jamaica was so decisive for us, as a family, but this was the new wind I had felt blowing.

At some point Vidar said to him:

"If Elleke is really as you describe..."

Yes, this was the case, he was sure of that.

"Well, what are you hesitating about! Go for it, man! You have everything you have ever wished for in a woman! ... And since Elleke has three children already, she can certainly have one or two more."

Yes, he had thought of this himself too. He wanted very much to have children of his own.

"What will you say when I want three more children?" he asked me at Christmas.

"My life is going so miraculously, that I won't exclude anything any more, but let's start with one and see how we're doing as a family," I'd replied smiling.

Vidar would have been so happy for him. And he would have been such a wonderful father.

I enjoy these stories. I always had the feeling Vidar and I were cooperating very well.

He also says that he saw how much difficulty Hermod had with daily hassles. When he shared Hermod's apartment for a while, this became even more obvious. He could withdraw for hours, because he had to make a phone call, calling me, for example.

"To be able to live with him, you really need to love him very much and be able to accept him as he is and stand firmly on your own feet."

This was clear enough to me.

"He could take half a day to wash his car, but he also took half a day when you came to him with a problem. He was very good to have as a friend. But he had no idea of time. Once I was mad at him, because he arrived far too late as usual. I said he would even be late for his own funeral. This is what is happening right now."

It is almost comic.

I talk about Jamaica and about the affection he had for Vidar, which I always sensed and noticed. It is strange to talk about him like this, while I have the feeling he is hearing us. But we are talking with love. We share, to bring us closer to him. We look at pictures and listen to the tape with his travel account. We cry and we laugh.

On Thursday we shall go to Kreatek, a centre for art and creativity, where he often went and where he had friends. He had wanted to take me there several times, but it had not happened yet. Vidar will tell the others that I am coming and asks me to bring the pictures and the tape with me.

When he leaves he says:

"I am afraid of you."

"What?"

This turns out to be a mistake in communication, due to the language barrier. He corrects himself immediately:

I am worried about you, how you'll be."

"I don't know either," I say, "I have no idea."

We embrace and say goodbye.

Anja, Cathrine and I have been invited for dinner by Jan Marcus, Beate and the nephews. I have decided to distribute the eleven troll children among all nephews and my children. I bring three trolls, together with the wallets I bought in Jamaica, presents and two of his frisbees. They jump at us and embrace us heartily. When we spent New Year's Eve together in the mountains we got to know each other a little better. They are so sweet. For them it is sad to have lost their uncle and hero. We sit around the table like a big family. It becomes a warm and sad evening. We cannot really think or talk about anything other than him.

The next morning is spent quietly at home again. Apart from the gatherings with the family, I do not feel like anything other than resting and pondering.

In meditation I am with him and actually I do not want anything other than this. We dance and fly around in a world of light, unearthly colours and transparent forms. I am in a state of absolute wonder about what I experience and what happens to me, feeling like Alice in Wonderland. I do not interpret, I do not question, I have no words for what I see and experience.

But besides this euphoria of freedom, I am now and then aware of his despair and sadness. I start to realize that although he is 'lighter' and in closer contact with his soul, in which he lifts me up and takes me with him, he still has his emotions and thoughtforms which need to be processed.

When I am with him we experience the joy of being together. These experiences expand me, they are healing, and make the pain more bearable, but they do not diminish it. On the whole I am being torn apart by sorrow.

He feels this, he is aware of us, who love him. He feels when he is being thought of. At that moment a connection is made and he is there. He now lives in an inner world, where thoughts and feelings are the only reality. For him there is no time or space limitation. I even assume he can be at several places at the same time, when more people think of him. He is very concerned about all of us. Besides this he has his own pain as well.

In the afternoon we select flowers for the funeral and Knut, Christiane, Jan Marcus and I go to the chapel for a last farewell to his body. We are all tense. It must be even more difficult for them than for me, I have already seen his body and said goodbye to it. And to me he is still there, and not in his body any more. Yet it still hurts, a sharp and cutting pain.

Hand in hand we enter the chapel. There he lies, but it is not him any more. After more than a week the body is like a fallen leaf, white and vulnerable. His wounds hardly show any more. He lies in a white coffin, in his white shirt, the shirt I had delivered. Weepingly we say goodbye, each in our own way.

Christiane and I lay an orange rose on his breast. And I lay Yoram's drawing of the tree of life at his feet, together with a mandala Tara made for him, and light four colourful candles, bought by the children.

We drive back in silence.

The following day, the day before the funeral, Anja goes back home. I have changed my flight, because of the postponement of the funeral. She is in the middle of her graduation and we have already been here for a week. I am grateful for her support thus far and feel strong enough to stay here on my own. Besides, I am not alone, among his family and friends.

Today I have made an appointment with Jørn, a friend, whom Hermod and I met at the course with the Dalai Lama. This is not so long ago, and although he is touched, he is not so filled with sadness as everybody here. This helps me too, it is uplifting to talk about other things for a change. He picks me up and we take a long walk through the forest, my first outing since I've been here. Just being together and the physical exercise of ploughing through the deep snow are of benefit to me. The forest is magnificent, white and silent.

In the evening Vidar picks me up to go to Kreatek. When we arrive they have just started with a short meditation. There are three empty chairs in the circle, one for Vidar, one for me, one for Hermod. On his chair are a cloth and a clown nose. He often played a clown to show the humour and sadness of human existence. Christian, a friend of his whom I have met before, gets up to greet me. Gunnar, another friend, whom I have not met yet, does the same. Silently we embrace and we take our places in the circle. After a short introduction we start with a warming up to music. Slowly we surrender our bodies to movement, emotions are being translated into body language. There is one overruling emotion which we share. We dance alone, together with changing partners. Sometimes we stand still in an embrace filled with tears.

Here I dance, my love, where you had wanted to bring me. Among your friends, in your place. I dance and I am.

Briefly we share in pairs our experience and then everyone can do whatever they feel like at that moment. There are facilities to paint, to write poetry, to play drama, to play music, to dance. It ends up as a collective jam-session with African drums. Sadness and powerlessness are beaten out.

Towards the end of the session we are left in the music room with three women. One woman softly starts to hum a song, another joins in. When the melody has faded away, a song bubbles up inside of me. I start to sing and my heart opens up.

I am singing for you, my love. My shyness and insecurity, which you found so endearing, but which you, with your overwhelming expressivity, helped me to overcome, have disappeared.

A memory comes up:

One day we were driving through the mountains and he wanted us to sing together, but I did not dare to. At a certain moment he stopped the car along the road and asked me to close my eyes.

"I'll bring you to real singers and when you listen attentively, you can sing along with them, if you dare to."

Carefully he led me, with my eyes closed and on bare feet, over stones, grass and then I had to squat down and listen. A deep buzzing at all pitches sounded in my ears. A bee colony!

Softly I started humming deeply in my throat. In the evening we sang together in front of the fireplace.

Now I am singing in Dutch and I feel safe among these people. It sounds clear, until my voice gets lost in tears.

Then it is finished. I go to the kitchen to get something to eat. Together we finish and listen to the tape and I show them some pictures. Vidar reads out two beautiful poems he wrote for and about Hermod. Tomorrow we shall see each other at the funeral. Christian brings me home, and I fall exhausted on the bed. I could not have spent this day in a better way. By singing and dancing, some of my pain has been acted out. I am ready to face the world tomorrow.

The day of the funeral. I am ready for it, but I do not want it. It is a ritual, it is only his body which will be burned. I feel him in my heart, I see him around me. But I do not want what is going to happen today. I do not want what has happened. Yet is has happened and this day belongs to it. That is how it goes in life. Abandoned bodies are burned or buried.

I spend the morning alone at home. I meditate and feel that we are together. The separation between our worlds is just an illusion, but it is a painful one. It is as unreal to him to experience this event. We communicate without words. I feel him inside like I feel myself. I had always thought that our communication would become like this, we have always been able to feel inside of each other. Though I never thought we would live in different dimensions like we do now.

Towards the end of the morning I fetch the roses I had ordered from my children, my mother, Anja and myself. We gather at Knut's place. Knut tells me that he will talk about the change he noticed in Hermod during our relationship in his speech. He had seen that his heart had become lighter and he is convinced that this was because he had found a partner who loved him and understood him. I listen with tears of emotion. Already. How do I get through this day?

Outside the chapel it is busy. We greet friends and family and we go inside. At the entrance are three big men, somewhat shy, each of them with a small present in his hand. Christian, Gunnar and Vidar:

"We have a small present for you. These are the birthday presents for Hermod, but we did not see him before he left. Now we would like to give them to you. You may keep them or lay them with the coffin, whatever you feel is right."

I open them, it is a clown's nose, a piece of crystal and a tiny pot of tiger balm, symbols of humour and creativity, clarity and strength. Wonderful wishes for a birthday and for a funeral.

I lay the roses in front of the coffin. The four candles from the children have been lit again.

We sit with the family in the first row. The chapel is plain, made of rough natural stone. In the flickering lights of many candles it is like a huge cave. Around the coffin it is a sea of flowers. It is beautiful. It is painful.

I cannot contain it. All impressions are coming in fragments. There is music by Bach, there is singing, the priest conducts the ceremony. Everything is in Norwegian, we had agreed on that. I can follow the main line, but I am distracted. Behind me the nephews are sobbing. Frederik cries a bit now and then and we take him in turn. I miss my children. They should have been here now.

Jan Marcus makes a speech. Then it will be my turn, if I have a voice. I try to gather my strength. Suddenly he turns to English and thanks me for what I have given Hermod. Please don't, for then I'll have to cry! My tears have dried up just in time when he finishes and it is my turn to speak. I pass the coffin, walk up to the platform, and look into the huge empty space of the chapel, to all the people who have gathered here for him.

For a moment I close my eyes and I can feel him.

Briefly I sketch his words on our last afternoon, about timelesness and paradise and that he would not mind dying now that he knew how beautiful life could be. I say that I found the text reflecting on his attitude towards life – the continuity of life. I read the text as a gift from him and me.

When I step down from the stage, Knut stands up to embrace me. The ceremony continues with music and a song. I am not able to listen attentively any more.

Outside the chapel we are greeted and embraced, people introduce themselves. Appearances, faces, eyes, people coming and going. I meet people and look into their eyes.

The reception is held in the restaurant of an attractive museum for modern art, sited along the fjord. This is the place where Hermod took me on my very first day in Oslo. After the visit to the museum we sat near the water, watching out over the fjord and he treated me to a delicious lunch in this restaurant.

Now we are here.

Cathrine and I walk for a bit along the water, or rather: the ice, before we go in. Inside we take a seat near the tables. Speeches from friends and family follow. Jørn, sitting next to me translates here and there, whenever I miss the subtleties. Out of all the stories it becomes clear to me how much he inspired people, and how gifted he was, in the eyes of others, in capturing ideas into words.

As an aunt of his says:

"He lives on in his ideas, with which he inspired us. Maybe that is why he was here."

Somebody reaching high and wanting to bring heaven on earth. It reminds me of the story he told me, a few weeks ago, about a lecture by a professor, to which he had been invited. The professor had given a speech which impressed everyone except him. He had some questions that none of his table companions could answer either. Finally he addressed the professor, followed by a discussion. The gentleman was so impressed by Hermod that he invited him to take over one of his following lectures on any topic he chose. He said he had seen the light around Hermod as soon as he had entered the room.

I also saw this light around him and still see it.

Of course his struggle with life is mentioned as well, one cannot talk about him without mentioning his quest.

One says 'nothing but good about the dead'. Now I see him in his essence, I wonder if this saying results from the fact that someone who has passed manifests more of his core, something which the relatives perceive, either consciously or subliminally.

Gradually people say goodbye. When I am talking with some friends a beautiful woman joins us, introducing herself to me as his ex-girlfriend. I am surprised, for I did not know she has been here all day.

"How special that you have come."

"Yes, it would be unnatural not to be here."

Cautiously we exchange. I feel there is some peculiar kind of kinship and affection between us. This day is a strange experience for her as well, although their relationship lies in the past and for years she has had another relationship. While talking, I sense a remnant of pain in her words. They had both been hurt.

I see him standing beside me and listen and I think I feel what he wants to say:

"Yet he had no reproaches towards you any more. He had let go and what remained was a warm feeling."

"It was good to be here and to hear all the stories which have brought some of the good memories of the time we had together to the surface."

I am happy for that. Maybe something has been healed between them. The conversation continues with questions back and forth until we heartily say goodbye.

Only the family is left. We select the flowers to take with us, as tangible, yet transitory reminders of this day.

At home I lie on the couch in my long black dress in between the flowers.

"Never before has your apartment been so beautiful... I wonder how this day has been for you. Due to all the tension I have hardly been able to feel you, apart from a couple of moments. It has been good. Today has shown how much you have given to people. A lot of love, inspiration and here and there pain as well. It was beautiful how their hearts were open, and how direct the contact was between people, some of whom hardly knew each other. Eye to eye with death and the vulnerability of life. You made quite an impression on so many people."

Wordless I feel his answer flowing into my mind:

"I know. I know what I have given to people, for good and for bad, and what people have given to me. More than ever I realize that life is worth living, because of human connections, because of love. A painful realisaton. I am touched by what I have witnessed today."

"I miss you, my love, and I am not the only one. You have a loving family and wonderful friends, who miss you as well. I wonder whether I do realize that you will not come back any more..."

When I step into bed, I suddenly feel him lying down next to me and putting his arms around me. It feels so authentic and almost physical, like that first night after the accident. We lie in each others arms and communicate wordlessly. Fulfilled I fall asleep. When I wake up at night, he is still there. All night I am aware of his cherishing presence.

As soon as I wake up in the morning I sit down for a meditation. Our communication works best when I have rested, am clear in my mind and able to focus. He pulls me out of my body and we dance until I cannot hold my concentration any more and sink back into my body.

I continue to feel his presence inside and around me, as if I am two souls, using one body. It is a peculiar feeling, a pregnant feeling. I think about it, could I be pregnant? No, very unlikely. Probably it is our connectedness which makes it seem as if he lives through me.

Today I want to be completely on my own. I have had several invitatons from friends and family, but now I do not want anything, maybe tomorrow. I enclose myself in the apartment, read and write a bit, rummage around, listen to music and do nothing.

In the evening I start to feel lonely. It is not easy to accept that our love cannot flourish any further here on earth. You are there and I am here. I cannot creep into your arms physically and we cannot dance in the ocean, only in our minds and our hearts. My heart feels big, bigger than my chest, because you are living within me. We talked about me creeping into your heart, this seemed better to you than the pain you felt so often in your heart. You allowed me to creep into your heart and you have crept into mine.

Now my heart is aching. If it stopped beating, I would not mind. Through this event I have become another woman. I have found my inner pearl, lived out my childhood's dream, experienced unconditional love and surrender and I have had to let go. Where do I go from here?

As long as I live, I wish to live with my heart and to give from my heart.

I want to give to the children from the pearl.

I sit down and relax. He is there and pulls me out of my body. It becomes familiar. We embrace and kiss. He takes me to a wonderful garden, which I am sure he creates for me on the spot. I am not sure whether I see the same garden as he does and this does not matter. It is beautiful and surreal. Now and then I question my perception.

"Do not doubt, it is unlimited here. The only limitations are those of your own reality frame."

I try to comprehend what this means. He takes me to his mother, who passed eight years ago. I have had an experience of meeting her soul before, even before I had ever seen a picture of her. We know each other. She seems to be doing fine. She lives a life similar to an earthly life, but now she creates it herself, in rest and peace. Besides she is connected with her family and her husband, who are left behind. She is happy that they are doing all right. She is also happy to have Hermod with her, although she is concerned about his pain. The pain of his life and his longing to be with me.

The communicaton between them stretches out beyond my comprehension. I am aware of my limitations, which is very frustrating, yet I am grateful that I am able to experience at least a glimpse of his world. We are together for a timeless time and then say goodbye to her.

We have not covered this explicitly, but I know there are more souls that he is in touch with, although I cannot perceive them very clearly. I feel that he also gets support and guidance from higher evolved beings. From the moment of his passing he has been going through his own process, which I catch only glimpses of.

He takes me by the hand in order to travel further. However I get tired and he brings me back to my body.

The last day in Norway and I feel miserable. I spend the morning packing and sorting things out. Rummaging around in the apartment I realize once more what a complicated person he was. His house reflects this with all its chaos and stuff kept for years. It is as if I lovingly move around in his unconsciousness. He has allowed me inside him, I would prefer to sort out his things. Like a sort of aftercare. It is hard to leave the apartment like this. But this is something to do with the whole family. And there is no time right now, I have to leave tomorrow. They have told me to take whatever I like. I choose some music and books, books we have discussed, on topics we shared – healing, psychology, philosophy, personal growth, science and spirituality. And I take a few personal things, like the troll children for Yoram, Tara and Imre, a frisbee and presents I gave him, or he gave me, but bought the same for himself, like the shellboxes.

I find the books he had bought for Imre, the plane we had bought together last year for the nephews and presents, presumably for little Frederik and his brother Axel. I select some pictures of our time together to give to Knut, together with his personal papers, address book, watch and presents for the nephews. I throw away some mail, mainly letters from me.

For the afternoon I have decided to combine two invitations and to visit friends in their unique house on a peninsula in the fjord. We have a lovely afternoon.

I am invited to dinner with Knut, Christiane and Cathrine. We discuss practicalities. We are together, but do not have much to say any more. It is enough to be in each other's company. Knut and Christiane like to go to bed early. Cathrine and I go out for a concert, which turns out not to be on, but we have a cosy evening anyway, walking and talking through the snowy streets of Oslo, and a cup of tea and chocolate at her place.

At home I sit down and we are together again. He is sitting in front of me and lays his head against my breast. My breast feels warmed by his touch. I do not believe my eyes and open them. It does not make any difference, I still see him and feel his touch.

"I love you more than ever."

"My love for you is stronger than ever too."

Both of us have been changed by his passage. We have become more aware of our core and see each other more in essence. The love is unlimited, unclouded.

"You are beautiful. You are like a flower... and this flower will bear fruit."

As soon as he says so I feel the different layers of my being opening up like petals, as if he touches me in different dimensions. I feel what he means, by our love I can continue to flourish. In this way he can live through me.

The next morning I pack my last things and go to Knut's apartment. Christiane is going home today as well and Knut will take us to the airport.

At the airport he treats us to coffee and buys some marzipan for me and the children. We say goodbye on the spot where I said goodbye to Hermod two months ago.

"There is no time," he then said.

"But life is short," I answered.

"That's true."

As soon as we pass through the gate I burst into tears. Another goodbye. When shall I come back here? And how different that will be...

5

Unity

Closing my eyes
you pull me out
of my body
Together we are
One
We travel
through timelessness, spacelessness,
gardens of eternity
With our golden bodies,
spiralling in our love,
we melt into each other,
One

Then I fall back
into time and space
my body
torn apart
pain
unbearable
We are One

yet apart...

Home, March

It is not easy to be back home. I am forced to deal with things I do not want to face up to yet. And the children make a justified appeal for my attention, while I am not fully present yet. I am getting support from all sides, friends, family, neighbours, clients and students, Hermod's friends and family. It helps, it does me good, yet I still have to go through my own process and bear my own pain.

I am taking it easy. I allow myself not to feel I have to do anything. I do not even have to try to be strong, to have to work, or to prove anything. I just try to be there, be there for the children and to do the daily things: preparing food, taking the children to school, making pancakes together, reading them a story, playing a game...

Rest and serenity have emerged, such as I have never experienced before. There are no 'have-to-do's', no fears, no uncertainties, no wishes, no longings.

I notice I can still enjoy the children, nature, being with friends, music, all kinds of things. But I feel naked and vulnerable like a baby, as if I have no skin any more. And I have pain, so intense that it tears me within. It is like a big open wound. My heart is aching. Everything I see around me reminds me of him. I dream of him every night. And time and again the image of the moment he was hit and taken by the car and how I found him on the street appears on my retina.

I get my strength out of our love. This is still there, this has not disappeared. I feel him inside and around me. Occasionally he appears all of a sudden, sometimes I can only see him, sometimes we can communicate. And in every meditation he takes me with him into his world and then we are truly together. I live in several realities simultaneously, which is a richness, but it does not make it easier for the time being. I need alignment in order to be fully present in life. And I feel torn apart by my longing to be with him and my sense of responsibility to be here and make the best of it, to manifest our love in life and to give to others.

Meanwhile daily life takes its course. I am finding my balance back with the children and we are doing well together. Despite everything it is cosy at home. There is an atmosphere of ease and intimacy, which he enjoyed so much when he was with us. They have their sorrow and I have mine. Sometimes we talk about it, not always. I am alert to the signals they give out. Their life mainly continues as before, since we were not living together yet. Nevertheless they gradually had come to think of him as their father and now they are going through their own grief. Yoram and Tara would have preferred that we were married, so our bond would have been confirmed officially and he really would have been their father.

Tara says:

"I had wanted to get to know him much better, but already I loved him so much. To me he was my father already."

Bit by bit they want to hear details about the accident. Imre starts talking about him a lot. Repeatedly she says:

"When Hermand was still alive ..."

She wants to be with me continuously and cries a lot. One afternoon we are having lunch in the garden. She says thoughtfully:

"Now we will never all be together again, for Hermand is not here any more. There is only Elleke, Yoram, Tara, Imre and Peter....."

I take Yoram and Tara horse riding. While riding, a child calls to another:

"Pim's rat is dead!"

"Pity!" the other calls back sympathetically.

Lightheartedly they ride on. That's life.

'Elleke's boyfriend is dead!'

'Pity!'

For others life goes on, no matter how empathic they are.

Cautiously I start working again, strongly determined to take as much rest as necessary. Through the intense experiences of happiness and pain I feel a compassion I want to share.

The first clients bring flowers and sweets. One of them, a sculptor, offers to make a bronze sculpture. He designs a round disc with two streams, merging together in a hole in the center and emerging as one on the other side. With an inscription in

Hermod's handwriting, derived from the fax he sent me on my last birthday:

'Jeg ønsker deg fra hjertet alt godt i tidløshet'

'I wish you from my heart all good in timelessness'

It is signed by both our names, his name in his handwriting, my name in mine, for now it is also my wish to him. There will be two sculptures, one for his grave, one for my home.

I shall use the space I create for myself for writing. All this needs to be written down, I cannot do otherwise, it needs to be expressed in words in order to ground my experiences, to ground myself, it is healing. And it is to honour him, to honour our love, and who knows, it may benefit the people around us.

His friends and family as well as mine keep in touch. Almost daily I get mail, flowers and phone calls from all over the world and from very nearby. I feel carried by a web of fine threads of interconnectedness. All the contacts are intense and open.

A Danish friend of his says that he often talked about death – something we all know he did – and that he told her he would stay in touch with us, if he were to die early. She said she had never believed in life after death at all, until Hermod died. She is sure she feels him around now and then...

A friend from Sweden calls. She says that, for the last year, he could only talk about me and he was very aware that I was his great love and that for the first time in his life he could, maybe, say yes. This was half a year ago. When she heard he was going to Jamaica with me, she knew he had chosen.

"Now he has left the earth with a positive purpose, which he had been looking for all his life," she says.

More friends of his have expressed this. Finally he learned to trust life, as he said on our last afternoon.

This is what he wrote to me half a year ago on a card which he left when he went back to Norway:

'Dearest Elleke,

I thank you from the heart of my being
for guiding me with your wisdom and enthusiasm
towards faith.
I love your graceful being,
Hermod
'Varm klem' (warm hug) to you all.
PS. This is a little present for everything and your birthday.

The question remains for all of us, then why did this have to happen?

We shall never know.

Often he is with me. Sometimes I notice before I see him, by the way my body reacts. My body, my whole being opens up to him, as it has always done under his touch or attention. Now and then he lies next to me, when I wake up in the morning, and it is almost a physical experience.

It is real to me and yet I doubt.

I remember one of the last days in Jamaica he gave me a magazine he brought from home on instrumental transcommunication, communication with the deceased via instruments. I had only taken a glance at it, my attention was focussed on other things at that time. What about it now? Our communication is there, it is substantial, but I doubt with my conditioned, logical mind... Shall I contact this organisation?

"You don't need that. You hear me straight, don't you?"

He answers my unspoken question.

Still I feel uncertain.

"Give me one signal!" I ask him one evening before I go to bed. "Just one clear instrumental signal, please. It is so difficult to trust from this side. You remember this, don't you? You with your scepticism have asked for signals too, before you were willing to accept something."

That night our travel alarm clock, which stands beside my bed, rings. The alarm is off, as it is the weekend. I check the alarm time, which is set on the weekly getting-up-time of 7am, not 3am. I get a light shock. Has our dear alarm clock broken down already? Or is this your signal?

It is as if he smiles.

Never again has the alarm clock rung at anything other than the set time, with the alarm set to go off, and it has always woken me up at the right time.

I am walking on my own along the beach and suddenly he is walking beside me, with his bouncing long steps. He looks at me and takes my hand. It feels so real that I put my physical hand in his as well. But the hand he takes is not physical and my physical hand makes a loose movement in the air.

"I hate it that you have no body!" I say frustratedly and half laughingly at the same time. He smiles too.

It is so absurd and weird and at the same time it feels so natural, the way in which we are still together. Pain and joy lie close together.

When I teach, he sometimes sits beside me. Some participants perceive him too. I almost feel like putting out an extra chair. He talks inside me, or adds something to what I say. It is confusing to intertwine this with what I want to say. Yet he does inspire me, as he has always done and I am aware of his gifts to me.

In meditations he takes me with him to the most unimaginable and surrealistic landscapes, sometimes comparable with the beauty of nature on earth, sometimes not comparable with anything we know on earth. In that reality one can create according to one's imagination. And he has always been very creative, one of the things I admired very much in him. Now he magically manifests the most beautiful gardens for me and enjoys surprising me. However, often I cannot hold my concentration for that long and occasionally I fall back.

With these ways of being together I do not miss him all the time. Missing him goes up and down. Somehow we have come closer than ever, two souls in one. But thinking of the future hurts, the realisation that he will not come back. All the things we could have shared.

Now and then there are spurts and bursts of uncertainty about our relationship. We were like this at the very beginning when it was good, wonderfully beautiful between us, but not easy. And probably it would not have been easy in the future either. But we wanted to go for it. Now we have not had the chance to work things out. I am forced to stay behind with sadness, anger, uncertainty and doubts.

I sit down to take it with me into meditation.

He sits down in front of me. I stay within my body and start to talk.

"Both of us were afraid to give ourselves. If I had been less afraid of your fear, whether you would be able to give yourself, I could have let you be more free."

"Don't mislead yourself by the limitations which life on earth brings along and which life has brought for us. Our fears and uncertainties were human. It was good between us, it is good and it will always be. Do not question that. That is not necessary any more. Life is grace. Your strength and beauty are within your true self."

"That is beautifully said and I know you're right, but you do remember how difficult it is to live accordingly, don't you?"

A smile with a dash of self-mockery:

"Yes, I know too well. But we can still work things out together, by sharing and forgiving. This is a healing process for both of us. You have your thoughts and emotions, I have mine and we are connected by many fine threads, some of which, the most essential ones, will remain, our love, the connection from heart to heart. Our souls will remain connected. But each of us has our own shadowsides and we can help each other to heal by acceptance and forgiveness, towards each other as well as to ourselves. We can dissolve painful connections by acknowledging what we have learned from each other and letting go of what has limited us."

I understand what he means, what he says goes beyond

words. We sit down for a meditation together.

I lay down the remnants of my doubts and uncertainties in front of him, as well as remnants of anger, because of his irritations, his resistance and my anger because he has left me behind here. He sees it and receives it. There is no judgement, only acceptance and I feel freed from a burden. Simultaneously he lays down his resistances, fears and defences in front of me. I receive them and try to stay focussed in my love for him, without judging or doubting. The whole process takes place in silence, we see each other's emotions and thoughts. Differences of opinion and tensions from the past pass by, are relived. Pain, fear, sadness, not necessarily between us, but merely within each of us and which have been expressed in relationships with others, with life in general, are being healed.

Now and then I am disturbed by his strong emotions, which come over me like wild storms. But my insecurity, emerging from my own emotions, works like oil on fire. There are fits of a wordless fight. Still we succeed in dissolving the storms in love, forgiveness and acceptance, by seeing each other in our essence, as a soul. We free ourselves and each other until we sit facing each other naked and defenceless. I know we shall do this more often. Bit by bit layers of destructive thoughts are being dissolved.

In a silent embrace we say goodbye.

I am deeply impressed.

During our stay with the Dalai Lama we had once bowed to each other, out of respect and unconditonal acceptance. What went on inside us was somewhat similar to this process. Often with him I have had the feeling that we are allowing each other to look inside at our full vulnerability. But what is happening now is beyond all normal human communication. Or is this human communication in its full potential?

In the evening I sit down to be with him and close my eyes.

He is standing in front of me and I want to jump out of my

body in order to go with him, but it does not work.

"Align yourself with me, receive me."

I relax and try to do so. Then I am pulled out by him in a blink.

Suddenly I understand how it works. It is as if his energy is lighter than mine. When I tune in to him, my 'frequency' is altered and it works by itself. With only an effort of will from my side nothing happens.

We kiss, dance and fly.

"I want to make love to you!" he says, while letting go of both my hands and pulling me close.

I am completely surprised. I can feel his longing, but there is nothing physical. We only have our lightbodies.

"Well, yes, how are we going to do this?"

"I'll show you..."

He embraces me and I feel his love penetrate my being. Our hearts touch each other. I surrender to my love for him. We feel inside each other. The borders of our lightbodies fade away, we expand to two big golden fields of light and merge together. We are one.

There is nothing short of us being one. It is ecstasy without orgasm. It is sexuality in its most subtle expression. We had touched upon this when we were both in a physical body. Now it is unlimited, more essential...

"I am so happy that you can come to me this way! You really are ... an inexplicable woman!I want to marry you."

"What?"

"I want to marry you."

I am really going mad, I think. I look at him, his face as serious as can be. This is real, I realize. He reads my thoughts. I feel a slight sadness in him, but also understanding for my reaction of disbelief.

"What does this mean? That I'll stay faithful to you like a widow for the rest of my life?"

"It means a connection, a commitment on a soul level. Nothing more and nothing less. Both of us will stay free in our own reality. Soul-connectedness does not exclude other love."

"Why didn't you stay alive, if you want to marry me?"

"During my life I was about to commit to you. That point of surrender and trust that I reached in this life, I can continue in another reality. By my transition I have come to a deep realisation of the worth of our love. I want to be with you in timelessness."

"I want to be with you too..."

Timeless we stand in each other's arms.

"You still have things to do."

"What then? Do you think I can still be happy here without you, after all you and I have experienced together?"

He smiles and says teasingly:

"No, now you may spend the rest of your life craving for me!"

This is the kind of humour I know of him, but I feel uncertain about what he means. He puts his arm around me and says:

"Don't be uncertain. I'll help you on your path..."

I feel he knows more than I do, but it is not for me to know this now. I have no access to his knowledge on this point. But I know his sincerity and I trust him completely. Although somewhere I still doubt my experiences with him. Deep inside I know, but Elleke is questioning. What is reality and what is imagination? I ask myself time and again.

"We create a reality together with our imagination and that is real."

Suddenly I understand it better. The three dimensional world is as much an illusion or a reality as this world. In our ordinary life on earth we each create our own subjective reality with our imagination. We think that reality is what we can perceive with our senses, but the human mind is reality. He inhabits the dimension of the mind. Because we are so connected on this level we have telepathic connection. We know each others' thoughts and feelings simultaneously. In this way we share a reality and create together, we co-create.

I become tired, lose my alignment and he brings me back to my body.

"Practise in silence and focus, so that we can be together and are able to travel together in this way. In this expanded reality we are always together. Do not forget that I am with you also when you are not aware of me. We are connected as souls."

Exhausted I sit on the floor.

When I wake up the next morning, I feel I do not want to live on. I had this feeling before, right after the accident. All the time I have put it away, for the children are there and I love them and I want to be there for them. And I have always loved life! Now the feeling is very strong. I want to be with him, in his world.

Unconsciously I have always known that this world exists and I have longed for it. It is a homesickness for where we all come from and where we shall all return one day. Even my love for the children cannot neutralise this longing. It is of a different kind. But is it not an illusion?

The sun is shining, birds are singing, spring is in the air. The children are playing sweetly. Sybille, a friend from Germany has come over to support me and stays overnight. That is all very nice, but I do not want to be here.

I realize I have given myself fully to him, with all I have and all I am. And he has given himself to me....

One day he had said:

"If I don't go for you this time, I'll die, not necessarily immediately, but then I'll die without ever having given myself to anyone."

He died, but not without having given himself. We were just beginning, we are not at all finished with each other yet. Our intentions and longings are still there.

Besides my own longing, I also feel his. I am almost frightened of the pulling movement coming from him, for it feeds my own longing to leave here.

I feel guilty towards the children and towards life. I have

always loved life. That was one of the aspects he appreciated so much in me. I still love life, but it has been enough for me. Something has died inside, something is completed. Which, of course, does not prevent a new phase from beginning.

Anyhow, I have to get out of bed now. Actually it is a fine day and after breakfast, after a talk with Sybille and a meditation I come to some insight. I must allow this feeling to be there. It makes no sense to try to hide it away or to feel guilty about it. It is not bad to want to leave. I do not think of suicide, I would never ever choose to do so. It is about a fundamental choice for life... to surrender to life, to live to the fullest.

Whenever I die, sooner or later, we shall be together. And there is no time anyway. Maybe this meeting is a preparation for something beautiful, where we can be together in another reality, as he suggested more than once, when he was still alive.

During our relationship there had been moments of such an intensity, that I sighed that I was willing to die together at the very moment, I was so absorbed in timelessness and selflessness. But since we were alive, I said we might as well live together. He was delighted with this and said we complemented each other perfectly. In his darker moods he was concerned about me and wondered whether he was doing me good.

"You don't know how strong my resistance is," he then said.

"You don't know how strong my love is," I answered.

We were both more concerned about the other than about ourselves.

I had never seriously considered a life without him. The last stage of our relationship I didn't think about dying or losing him any more. I had joyfully wanted to die for him if this could free him from his existential pain. Now the challenge is to live for him joyfully. To stay with the essence of our love and to let go of him as well. Our connectedness will remain, as he says. But emotionally we shall have to let go at some point. This process will take time.

He says time and again:

"What is there between us, cannot but continue. Out of our love can only come something beautiful. We are together. Don't let yourself be misled by this illusory separation."

I feel this is true, but I struggle with the separation I experience between our worlds, even though I transcend this separation daily in meditation.

Shortly after the experience of our merging souls he takes me to a silver spring. he holds me and cherishes me. My lightbody, my whole being opens up. With our arms around each other we stand in the middle of a fountain of light substance. This substance sparkles and squirts around us and through us and feels very vitalising and transforming. I feel purified. Our lightbodies become golden and radiant.

Once more he asks me very seriously:

"Do you want to marry me?"

This time I have no doubts or questions. I feel the timelessness of our connection and know.

"Yes."

We make love in our lightbodies and merge. We are fully transparent and feel inside the other as within ourselves. There is such an overpowering love that I cannot contain it and almost faint.

When I am back in my body, I wonder how I can continue living on earth now I know that this is there. These experiences nurture me and transform me, but I am also being pulled away from the earth. I feel I have to go through this, I cannot ignore it, for I have always known that these worlds exist.

I remember past lives in which I was able to travel through other dimensions as well. It should be possible to integrate consciousness of other dimensions into a healthy, fruitful life on earth. But do I want this? Do I want to stay here at all?

I make a sequence of appointments with Joop, a good friend of mine, who is a psychotherapist, in order to help me get some clarity. He is objective and critical and can give me some counter-balance. We discuss the phases one goes through in a bereavement process, the outbursts of feelings, the phase of non-acceptance. It is all allowed to be there.

We discuss my experiences in an expanded reality, which we accept as my reality, my psychic inner world, without any judgment or generalisation to other people's realities. Joop helps me with his sharp questions to stay alert in distinguishing between my different perceptions.While acknowledging that I am in a process of grief, I try to distinguish who is talking. Is it my soul, or higher self, either in communication with Hermod or not, or is it my subconscious, or my emotions talking? I want insight into my deeper knowing and to understand it through and through. But it does not have to happen right now. I can take my time.

One afternoon Imre and I are having our lunch. I look at her radiant small round face, all zest for life and joy of life. What a wonderful being she is! I look straight into her soul.

"Imre, why have you actually come to earth?" I ask her curiously.

For a moment she looks thoughtful. Then she looks at me, with her wise, green eyes, smiles, and says:

"I don't know....to play!"

I could not have got a better answer.

"And you, Elleke, why have you come to earth?"

In the past I used to have a clear answer to this; to learn, to help...

"I don't know either, maybe also to play, and to teach others how to play..."

I do not have anything better to say. But I do not like the game any more without Hermod, I think inside. I do not want to play any more. And I feel guilty towards Imre and towards Yoram and Tara.

I know he is concerned about them as well. Sometimes I see

him around them. He does not want me to leave them. When I talk about this with my mother, it reminds her of his last words to her, when we phoned him on his birthday, shortly before we left for Jamaica. I was ill and in bed at that time.

"Drive carefully with the children through the snow!" he told her.

I know that eventually I shall have to let go of him, we shall have to let go of each other as personalities, for the people Hermod and Elleke will never be together any more. The souls we are will always be connected and there will be other forms in which we shall be together. But how difficult it is to trust this and to let go of my longing to be with him now.

Half a year ago he said:

"You are less dependent on me than I am on you..."

I had looked at him in amazement and he continued:

"I mean it! If we were ever to break up, I would not know what to do, but you would be able to continue your life and you would be fine."

I have to try.

6

Light

Penetrating
every cell of my being
Piercing
into my core

Consciousness

Revealing dashes
of the Unknown
Lightening my heart
Stripping skin
after skin
of defence
Until nothing's
left but naked

Self

April

Gradually, over the weeks, I am coming more down to earth and do not feel so entirely vulnerable and naked without a skin anymore. While he is drifting more away from the earth. He is less frequently around, I see his appearance becoming less physical. Though I can always sense him in my heart, when I align with him. When I want to feel him, it does not work. I cannot force the connection with my will. One time he even reacts somewhat irritatedly:

"You should not try to pull me towards you with your will! I am always there, you don't have to try to force me."

"Sorry, I apologise. I still need to learn how to deal with this. Now and then I feel so miserable, I just need you."

I feel his love as a stream reaching out to me.

"That's okay. I am there for you, as you are there for me. Just try not to use your will, you can ask me instead."

Often when I feel sad, he is there by himself, for he is aware of every connection being made with him by anyone.

To act out my pain, which is still flooding me daily, I often dance on my own in the evening, to one of his CDs. One evening, he joins me and is physically so very much present, that I tend to put my arms around his neck, which I do, in the air. Together we dance the whole CD to the end. It is wonderful. Afterwards, when I go upstairs, he follows me as if it is most natural. It confuses me, this life with a ghost. Sometimes he is only present in my meditations, when I am clearly aligned and at other times, like now, he is unexpectedly around in an almost physical shape and we can just talk normally.

It is getting too much. I do not know what I trust of my feelings and perceptions. I sit down on the floor of my work room and start to cry aloud. He takes a place on the chair in front of me.

"...I still don't know whether we really have danced together or just in my imagination!" I desperately cry out.

"Haven't we danced together in our imagination and wasn't that real?" he asks gently.

He has said this before. Then he adds more persuasively:

"From now on you either think that you are crazy, or you accept that I am a reality!"

I look at him. That is a good point. I ponder on it and decide that I do not meet the criteria for psychopathology, according to the definitions in my textbooks. He is right. I should not question him and myself time and time again.

I give him a kiss (in the air). "Thank you, love, you are right."

And go to bed.

In meditation we still are together, but there is a gradual change in the quality. He takes me further and further and the experiences become more intense and more subtle. He transcends further and it requires more concentration and alignment on my part to be able to follow him. When I am too tired or too sad, or too eager, it does not work. A certain quality of mental clarity, silence and openness is needed to be able to receive him. He guides me and teaches me. I train my concentration and grow with him, so to speak.

I ask him what he actually does when I am not with him. He answers, but I can not hear him quite, because what he says goes beyond my understanding. In my reality frame there are no concepts to make sense of this information.

Then he shows me and takes me to some kind of psychological school, where he is a 'student' and I join in with his experience. It is a transparent building of light, looking somewhat like a temple, where beings, souls in all kinds of appearances, human and non-human, teach and receive teachings. Part of his education consists of being with his friends and relatives whom he has left on earth, partly to work things out, from which he has to learn himself, and partly to guide and support them. In doing so, he studies and processes life in general and the effects of his own life in particular. He is being guided in this process himself.

I can see it is the tragedy of many souls on the other side as well as of the living on earth, that the living are generally not conscious of their contact with souls who have passed on. The passed souls are thought of and cried for, as they were in life on earth, but they are being ignored in their present state of being.

When the physical dimension drops away, ie. when the person dies, the psychic dimensions of a person are often not accessible any more for the ones who stay behind and communication is no longer taking place. Sometimes because people who are left behind think it is not possible and do not even try, or sometimes because they are not able to make the necessary alignment and open up for another reality. Or it might be that many people do have some perception of contact with their loved ones, but do not trust these, since it is usually very subtle and not through our regular senses.

It may also be that it is the passed souls who may naturally move on to other realms from where they are less likely to communicate openly, although the love connection remains. And there might also be other reasons of which I have no understanding.

In any case it is supportive and healing for the passed soul to be thought of with love, in the way they are in their essential state of being, which is usually much more expanded than their expression on earth has been.

I realize that we are supporting each other mutually, by our love connection, and we are both grateful for this.

The magnitude of his education consists of – at least as far as I can perceive with my limited perception – the integration of his different personalities in different realities into one self.

He 'dissolves gradually' from being the person Hermod as he was in this life. (In truth I do not know what gradually means in our time, so I use the word metaphorically, since in that dimension there is no time and space as we know it).

I catch a glimpse of this, but am not able to grasp it mentally. He takes me with him in this experience. We travel through time and space and through this I experience myself more as a soul and experience glimpses of myself, my self in other personalities, in other realities. Here it seems we have transcended the lower, or more dense realms of illusionary forms.

Apart from all this he still regularly appears like Hermod, with all his sun and shadow sides.

"I am preparing a surprise for you," he says one day, *"for when you come."*

"For when I come?"

"Yes, for you are my wife now, aren't you?"

I do not know what he means, when I come in meditation, or when I die within whatever timespan, for there is no time for him.

A little later he refers to this surprise again and seems quite excited. I am getting curious.

Then, one time, he proudly takes me to a home he built himself. It looks as if it is made of white painted wood, but it is a transparent light substance. It is situated on a cliff, with verandas all around, looking out over the ocean. It looks a little bit like his family's summer house, which he loved very much, and it's also a bit like the place where we stayed in Jamaica, and yet it is different. It feels like home. I can see he has also thought of me in the design and interior.

"This is our house. You can always come here, when you are tired or sad, or want to be with me, or just to withdraw from life for a little while."

In my amazement I cannot say anything.

"I didn't know one could build houses here. Besides I thought you were gradually withdrawing from the sphere of illusionary forms."

"Here one can create whatever one desires. Many souls create their own home. And they behave like they used to on earth, for that is the reality frame they are familiar with. I can be present in different realms. This realm is a nice playground, to relax and to heal."

Now I remember that, when we visited his mother, she also lived in a house. But at that time I could not yet see very clearly.

Proudly he shows me around the house. There are some vague spots here and there, walls that are trembling, appearing and disappearing. I look at them in surprise, are they there or are they not?

"Ah, it is not quite finished yet. I haven't been able to make up my mind yet about some walls," he says lightheartedly.

I burst out laughing. Apparently he has not yet been able to get over this trait of indecisiveness. Luckily for him, in this sphere thoughts immediately manifest into form. This enables him to get things done, which would have been more troublesome in dense matter.

"You can build it as well, make it as you feel comfortable with."

A dreamhouse. All according to my wishes! What we wish manifests at once. Maybe we do not even see exactly the same house... each of us has our own reality. It does not matter. In any case we can share each other's reality to some extent and that is a privilege.

We sit down on the veranda.

"Would you like a drink?"

"A drink? Is that possible?"

"Everything is possible."

He gets up and I follow him to... there is no kitchen, I realize. He does not need one here.

"If you want a kitchen, then here is your kitchen!" he says casually.

In no time there is, instead of a wall, a rough impression of a kitchen, similar to the kitchen in his summer house. Out of nothing he takes two glasses, filled with something that looks like liquid. We walk back to the veranda, sit down in two lazy chairs and raise our glasses.

"To our being together!"

Cautiously I take a sip. It is delicious! It tastes similar to a mixture of piña colada and a fruit juice I like.

"You taste what you want to taste."

We are enjoying ourselves.

Then he shows me the bedroom and we tumble on the bed until I cannot hold my energy any more and am being vacuumed to my body.

It is a lovely idea to have a man and a dreamhouse near the sea. From now on I go there regularly in my meditations. Sometimes he is there, sometimes I am on my own. It is a nurturing base.

But how to continue in my ordinary life? When I do my daily things, my sadness is no less. I yo-yo up and down between highs and lows. It is the end of April and he would have been here by now, to stay for a month. The weeks without each other would have been over already.

On the inner plane I experience a freedom I have always longed for, but the price is high, for the pain of the division is unbearable. I can only bear it by transcending duality, which happens in meditation. I get my strength out of this... or does it pull me away from life?

One evening he suddenly appears in front of me, puts his arms around me and takes me with him. We ascend at high speed through subtle dimensions. The 'frequency' becomes so high, that I feel my being can hardly bear it, it's as if I am exposed to high voltage. It feels as though I am going to faint. He holds me more firmly and takes me further. I have complete trust that he knows what he is doing. I feel his love enclosing me and try to surrender, letting go of any thoughts and questions.

A blinding bright light appears, the brightest and strongest light I have ever experienced. No, it does not appear, it has always been there, it is we who appear in this light now. It is light penetrating my being into each cell, each vessel, as if I am being scanned into the deepest core of my soul.

The light is consciousness, it is love, it knows me better than I know myself.

Hermod is still holding me. We are standing as souls intertwined in the light, in void, emptiness, vast space. Beyond time and space we see several universes, including our earthly universe, passing by in a magnificent development, unfolding throughout time.

There is knowing.

The magnitude is so overwhelming, too overwhelming, I almost succumb. He is standing upright and radiant. I realize he is better able to bear the light, because he is not bound to a physical body. Besides I know he has been here before. It is not a common place for 'mortal beings'.

We go further and further into the light. It purifies and nurtures me as a chastening fire, but the intensity is almost more than I can take. I can take it because he, as a soul without a body, is holding me, enclosing me with his love. I know that, if we go further, I will not be able to return to my body any more. The force and the love are so overpowering that I cannot but surrender, to him and to the light.

I sense his purity as I sense my own.

Then we dissolve. There is only light, unity, consciousness, love. Timeless silence.

Faintly I become aware of my identity again. The force becomes too strong. Weakly I hang in his arms. He carries me back to my body. Everything has happened in complete silence.

Now, back in my body, I mumble to him:

"... but I cannot leave the children behind. They should be here too..."

"I know. It's all right. Just take some rest now," he answers.

It costs a lot of effort to come back to physical reality. My head feels like bursting from pain and pressure. Tears of emotion are running down my cheeks.

After this experience I feel clearly that, as long as I live, I can only live in love. There is no other way. Otherwise I will not live. What I experience now can only be expressed, in all minor and major daily activities. Life may be beautiful, beyond my imagination. Yet now, life is painful.

May

It is the week of the retreat with Michael Roads, which we had wanted to go to together and had been looking forward to for a long time. In January he had said that our experience in Jamaica would be a good preparation for this retreat. Now I am going on my own. Yet I am not alone. The whole week he is with me, I sense his presence almost physically, and we do all the meditation exercises together.

It is a major challenge to be here, for my pain is still on the surface and intimate contacts elicit tears. At this retreat I am being challenged to live to the fullest, as self, as a soul, and this is exactly what I am struggling with. I want to and yet I do not want to live.

During the meditations I find more and more that it is not a matter of life and death, but a choice for truth, a choice to be me to the fullest and to follow my path, which is not necessarily the same as his.

He is more connected to his soul-consciousness than I am and most of the time I feel his support and guidance in my process. He entirely supports me in being here, with the children, in life. But it seems I also feel an undercurrent coming from him, I sense that he is longing for me.

I have sensed this ambivalence since the accident. It confuses me.

One evening I decide to ask him straight:

"What do you want: that I'll die soon and be with you, or that I continue my life? What do you really want when you try not to think what's in my interests or the best interests of the children."

He hesitates. I feel he does not want to influence me with his personal will.

"For me it is most wonderful when you are here. It is wonderful here, but together with you it is more wonderful. Yet I want you to lead your life according to your purpose and I want you to be happy. And I want you to guide the children on their path. I want to help you in this. For me there is no time, there is no short or long waiting. For me our separation weighs less than for you, because I am with you all the time."

"But you did not want to live for me, you'd rather die," I protest.

I know this is not fair, but I have to hear him answering this.

I am thinking of his words half a year ago, when he said: "Elleke, I love you so much, there are no words for! But still I can see no future in this life..."

"I did want to live with you and I wanted us to have a child together, but for a long time I didn't trust enough. I couldn't believe that I would be able to do this. You guided me towards trust and I was on my way. This death was not a choice of my personality."

"I love you more than my life," I tell him.

"I had often thought that I would die for you, or live for you and take over your existential pain. Now I have this pain. And I know I can transform this, if I dare to trust in myself, in life. Once we talked about unfolding our wings and conquering our fear of flying. I said I would fly, even when you wouldn't, because it is my purpose. Now I don't know where to fly – towards freedom, towards truth? Maybe I'll fly to you, who knows? I know you are making your flight now and in a way we are flying together."

"We are flying together! And we free each other with our love. By letting go of the pain of this illusionary separation and experiencing the unity of your soul and of mine, you free us both. Your pain is my pain. Your freedom is my freedom."

A flash of insight cuts through me, when I let these words sink in. This is what is happening! By our connection across dimensions, we can somehow share each other's growth process. Long ago I had a premonition that we would go through some kind of realisation together. Even then I had thought this would take us a whole lifetime together, if not more. Now it seems it is taking place anyway.

During the retreat we get a request for a meditation to try to meet someone who has passed. Hermod is there before the exercise has started. For a long time we stand in a silent embrace, as souls in our golden egg-shaped energy fields.

Tenderness.

"Are you coming?" he gently asks.

It is my own choice. Now I feel my longing to be with him at the core of my soul. It cannot be denied. It transcends life and death. Our love has a purpose in itself. There are things which we could not do on earth together, which we can do in another reality.

"Yes."

We amalgamate. At that moment, I get a sharp pain in my lower spine, which rises quickly. That is interesting, I note, never before have I had physical pain during meditation. I had already let go of my body. Now the pain has called me back. It spreads out and becomes more intense, it is like the last phase of childbirth. My lungs seem to collapse under high pressure and I notice my heart beat is wavering. I am about to faint. In amazement I realize that I might be dying.

This is not the time and the place, I realize. At that moment we are being told to come back and with the help of the voice of the person who is guiding the exercise, I come back with the greatest effort. With my head on my knees, I try to avoid fainting.

I realize the choice has been made. It is only a matter of time. Suddenly I feel guilty. I should not feel this. I should not want this. On the other hand I know these feelings are a natural part of a grief process. It is no use trying to hide them away. But with my experiences with Hermod, a totally new dimension is added, which everyone may query.

During the retreat it is a relief to be able to share some of my experiences with Michael and his wife Treenie who confirm a lot of what I tell them by their own experiences in other realities*. This is a support. I have decided to go for my own reality, my truth and search these experiences out to the core. Only in my core can I bring back my will to live.

My meditations become clearer and more intense. He is there and takes me with him: once we soar to the most subtle dimensions I can bear, where we are souls without a shape, just essence. Another time we stay in the realm of forms and colours.

It is not clear to me what determines this. There is no time in these realms, or at least, time is another concept. He exists in more dimensions simultaneously and is able to manifest anywhere according to his will. Or is it my projection and comprehension which determine what I perceive of him?

"Will this always be the same?" I ask him. I am referring to the infinity of this miraculous realm of illusionary forms. It is marvellous, but it is an illusion. The more subtle realms tend to appear more essential.

"We can decide that for ourselves. We can travel and learn endlessly in this realm. But we are here mainly for relaxation and healing."

I feel limited by my expectations and prejudices, yet despite that I feel the unlimitedness. I try to go with him actively, by willing myself to go forth, but this only achieves the opposite.

"Can you let yourself be guided by me?"

I relax and focus on my receptivity to his energy, letting go of all expectations. Then we can move freely. We fly across a universe of colours and unmanifested forms. He points to a golden island, which appears out of nothing. He is creating it.

"Over there we can rest a little bit."

I know this 'resting' of his. It is an old expression he uses for something else. I feel his longing, which surprises me every time. Making love is not something I think about when we are in this realm. But he has always surprised me. Slowly and intensely we make love within our golden bodies of light. Our souls are quivering together.

"You were right about the meaning of life. Life is meaningful and beautiful. And I was right about wanting to leave life. I was not able to experience this in life. I needed to go through this first."

"Are you still concerned with the suffering on earth or are you just enjoying this realm?"

"I am concerned about it. Now, by what we are going through together, I also have the intention to come back in another reality to share our qualities."

We play a little more. We dance freely and weightlessly and

create the most beautiful forms with our imagination and let them dissolve again. Then I get tired and have to go back.

Other times we fly above the Earth and travel through spheres of nature. We experience the consciousness of plants and animals.

One time we dive into the ocean and swim along with a group of humpback whales. The water feels like water, but in our light-bodies we can breathe freely anywhere and move freely at any speed we want. The whales are aware of us and we can communicate with them telepathically. I feel the magnitude of their consciousness. They are one in consciousness and do not experience separation. When a whale dies, they all stay consciously connected. They are able to withdraw their soul consciously from their body in order to choose to die. There is no judgement to this, for there is no separation between life an death. We can learn much from them.

These experiences expand and enrich me, but in between these flights I am flooded with very human feelings of pain and loss, waves of sorrow. The mornings are usually the most difficult for me. I often wake up sad. I question everything and I am angry about the loss that has happened to me. I start to talk to him aloud. At once he sits at my bed. I feel his concern about me. My pain is his pain. He is also concerned about the children.

"I want to take care of you."

He takes my lightbody out of my physical body and carries me.

While I am lying in my bed, I fall into meditation, something I have never been able to do before, as I always immediately fall asleep while lying down. Now I am wide awake. I feel a bit uncomfortable in his arms, afraid that I am too heavy.

"Let go! You don't have weight here, that's an illusion."

I realize how conditioned I am.

He takes me to a magical garden near the sea.

"Would you like to go into the garden or to talk first?"

"I'd like to go into the garden first."

He takes out a green dress, made of a smooth, silk-like fabric, for me, and a shirt and trousers made of the same substance for himself. Surprise! We dress in thse silken clothes, then we walk and enjoy the garden. There are dolphins coming into the bay and we swim with them. This is all a paradisical illusion which he creates to help me relax a bit.

"We can stay in this paradise for a timeless time."

"Shouldn't we do something useful?"

"That is always possible. There is no time here, you know. Besides, our love radiates out into the universe, that's a gift in itself."

Finally we sit on a bench. I do not need to tell him about my pain, my sadness, my longing and my struggle. He knows all of it.

"Trust! Stay with your own truth. With doubts or negative thoughts you undermine yourself, don't do that. Live your pearl! To me you're the most beautiful being in the universe. We can timelessly be together and I support you in everything. Don't doubt, trust!"

He carries me back to my body and when I open my eyes, he is still sitting next to my bed, holding my hand.

The next morning I wake up with an empty and sad feeling again. I call him and he is there, but I am still too tired. I am not able to focus yet and I get lost again. He is very patient and tries to hold my attention steady.

"Try once more. Align with me."

I try to align and we ascend, higher and higher, passing through more subtle realms. I realize he wants to bring me to the light once more. I had better sit up for this. I return to my body, open my eyes, and get up and go to the toilet first. Then I sit down on the floor of my work room wrapped in a blanket. He is still there. As soon as I close my eyes we rise again. The light becomes brighter.

"I bring you my wife," he says, while letting go of me and stepping back.

Now I am here on my own strength. The light penetrates me

fully. I am able to bear it better than the first time. I am being tested at the deepest core of my unconsciousness. A question rises in my mind:

"Do you want to die?"

I am aware of my deep longing to be united with him.

"Yes."

Suddenly he is being taken out of my consciousness. He is gone. There is nothing but light.

"Do you really want to die?"

I am aware of the many lines connecting me with life, the children, people around me. I realize I don't want to die.

"...No..."

The light expands and consumes me. I only know I want to be in this light. This is the One. This is beyond life and death, beyond my connectedness with the children, beyond my love for Hermod. This is universal love.

I choose for being in this light, just being, and I surrender all of myself. Everything is one.

Suddenly there is some awareness of 'I' again and I realize I am free and that he has made the same choice. In my mind I hear a voice:

"Your love has been approved, you'll be united."

At that moment I feel him standing beside me and we embrace, merge.

Gratitude.

He brings me back to my body.

I need to cry.

From the very beginning of our relationship I have had the feeling that we could bring each other to God, but I never quite understood what it meant. Now I do, it is what we have experienced now. We have transcended human love, into universal love, into oneness. There is no question any more about whether I want to live or not. I am living! I am. There is no separation. It is not up to me to decide.

I want to play the game according to the rules. My human vision contains only a minute fraction of the universe. I bow before a consciousness infinitely bigger than mine.

After this he brings me to the light a few more times, until I am able to get there on my own. I would prefer to stay in this state, but I cannot. It demands such a focussed concentration and clarity, which I cannot always summon, far from it. Besides, the challenge lies in experiencing the oneness in daily life. And this is difficult. Throughout the days I still feel torn apart and I am exhausted by the flood of emotions and the weight of ordinary daily hassles and responsibilities, no matter how gently I try to take it.

It is quite a task to integrate these spiritual experiences of existence with fiery human emotions. Emotions cannot be ignored either.

He still has his emotions as well. Once in my meditation I go to our home and find him there in a dense state. He is dwelling in apathy and frustration, because he is creating his reality in his realm as well as on earth and now he is not able to lift himself out of his limitations.

I am amazed that this is still possible after all our cosmic experiences of love and soul consciousness. Apparently these conditions remain, like my emotions of pain and loss, for as long as they are not completely dissolved, although the focus of consciousness shifts to more subtle realms.

The only thing I can think of is to bring him to the light. I gather my concentration and enclose him with my love. Gradually it feels as if the frequency accelerates and it becomes lighter around us. First he resists and shrinks.

There is a question in the light:

"Would you rather suffer or radiate?"

He looks behind, to me. I nod. Slowly he rises. The light penetrates him and now he shows his full potential and he is beautiful. He dissolves in front of my eyes. Now I am alone in the light.

"Do you doubt him?"

I look as deep and as honestly into my mind as I can, which is made easier by the light. And I admit that I did doubt him sometimes, when we were both living and he was lost in apathy and depression. Even now I sometimes doubt him. Yet deep in my heart I have always trusted and I was willing to go through all storms for him. I look straight into the light:

"I really choose for him, even if it takes lifetimes of struggle."

"Your love will be confirmed."

Suddenly it dawns upon me that his blockages exist in me as well. Doubting him is doubting myself in a masked form. There is no separation. What I see in him, exists in me, and vice versa. This is the potential we were both aware of in our relationship. The potential we have seen that encompasses the best and the worst qualities in each other. This is the potential of the Hermod-Elleke unit. This is also the potential of each of us individually, each human being and of relationships in general. But we do not have to struggle for lifetimes. We can free ourselves, release our potentials, now.

Happy I return to our home, where I find him. We evaluate our experiences. By seeing and respecting each other as a soul, and by confirming our essence, we support each other's growth as well as the liberation of each of us individally. By self acceptance and love we manifest our essence, our true self.

It is Mother's Day and the children give me sweet, handmade presents: paper bags from Imre, "to put something in", paper hearts from Tara, and a paper diamond and a paper treasure box from Yoram with the inscription:

"In this diamond you can keep your love for Hermod."

When I ask him how he came to this, he answers:

"I thought this treasure box is to keep your most precious things. What's the most precious thing you have? It's your love for Hermod!"

I am deeply touched by the wisdom and the empathic capacity of this ten year old child, but a little bit startled by it as well. Am I shortfalling in my love for the children? When I look honestly inside, the answer is 'no'. My love for them is clear and it is good between us. However it is love of a different kind, not less, but different. I love them and they are beautiful souls, each of them. They have come through me and I am responsible for them and I want to be there for them. Later they will lead their own lives.

This year in Yoram's class at school they study the Edda, the book of the old Germanic, Norwegian mythology. Now they are at the myth of Hermod, Odin's son, who travels to the underworld to plead for the return of his late brother Balder. He functioned as the messenger of the gods and was able to travel freely through the different worlds, like the Greek god Hermes. Hermod himself was happy with his name and the myth. He was a messenger of a higher world of ideas and inspiration. He still is. Yoram tells the myth to his teacher and it is discussed in the class.

At night, in bed, he says: "I wish I could travel to the underworld to plead for Hermod's return."

Since the accident he has been suffering from migraine-like attacks, when he cannot do anything but lie in bed. One morning at breakfast Imre asks:

"Elleke, can I leave my porridge? I have pain in my stomach."

"Yes, that's all right."

"Do you have pain in your stomach too?'

"Not right now, but I have had some pain in my stomach lately."

"Yes," says Yoram, " and I often have a headache. We all have pain because Hermod died."

"Ah, yes," Imre says solemnly, " that's why we are all so sad, but ..." she looks up radiantly and raises her finger wisely in the air and states: "He will be born again and then he will be zero!"

Imre often says to me:

"When we're dead, we'll still love each other, won't we!"

One morning, when she is about to take her bath, she jumps naked into my arms and says joyfully:

"Let's cosily die together, for then we'll be with Hermand!"

One evening Tara and I do some yoga exercises together, before I put her to bed:

"I have a good life," she says. "Actually some terrible things have happened to me: my parents are divorced and are not living together any more and my mother's boyfriend, whom I love very much, has died... that's even more terrible for you than it is for me. Those are terrible things and still I am happy!"

I realize that only when the children are grown up, will we really be able to have some insight into the depth of the wounds caused by these events.

Now as earthly time is going by I feel obliged to let go of him. This is stimulated by remarks from friends, his friends as well, saying that at some point I will have to let go of him. Vidar touches me by saying that all the energy I spend on Hermod, I am spending on death, which cannot be the meaning of life.

Is this true? I think I have to go through this in order to get back to life. Yet I doubt myself. It does not go without saying any more that Hermod is present in my meditations; and he does not take me out of my body that often any more.

When I am well aligned we can be together, but not automatically whenever I want to. I try to meditate more on my own strength, the way I used to do it before he passed. He usually appears sooner or later anyway, often unexpectedly:

"What about me?" he asks quasi-indignant.

"I am trying to let go of you. I am afraid I may be clinging to you too much, and that might hinder you in your development."

"We don't have to let go of each other, at soul level we can always stay together. And as personalities we'll let go of each other in a natural way, you don't have to force this. I want to take care of you now. I am

concerned about you, for I know how tough this is for you. This is not deducted from my development, which is yours as well. Your development is mine. You are freeing me with every step you make in your process. We need to play with attachment and detachment, remember?"

I remember a talk we once had about attachment to and detachment from each other. A burden is released from my shoulders. I realize that I have tried to banish him out of my system. I do not have to let go of him yet. Not even three months have passed. And even if it takes the rest of my life, so what!

"Come, we'll have a swim!"

And he pulls me through the illusory realm to a familiar beach. We dance and swim in the water and we are very close again.

"You need this. We are allowed to enjoy, you know. You are allowed to let all feelings just be there. Besides, I am longing for you too."

It is lovely and we are nurturing each other.

Another time, when I feel miserable again, he takes me to my guides. They are a group of souls, let's say friends, with whom I have been in touch for years and by whom I am being guided. Strangely enough, it has not come into my mind at all to get in touch with them during the past months. He takes me there now and we are in a circle with them. It is a warm reunion, although they have not lost sight of me.

There are two things that strike me. First, he is one of them now, he is radiant like they are and I feel his power is of a similar kind. But he is a special one, because we are partners too. I smile at the thought, for during his life he sometimes exclaimed in despair that my friends could give him a sign as well. Second, I see to my astonishment that my relationship with them has altered. Before I was like a toddler in their midst, equal in potential, yet in actual consciousness a child in comparison with them. Often I only understood a fraction of what they were talking about and I could hardly bear the light they were emanating. It was as if I were a toddler, coming out of my dark bedroom late in the evening, half asleep and entering the bright light of a huge room, full of adults, not being able to bear the light or to understand what was going on.

Now it is different. I am one of them in consiousness, although very limited in my human condition. But I feel their respect, because they know how the limitations of the three dimensional world veil pure consciousness. I have always felt their respect. Still it is different, I am not a toddler any more. They look at me with love:

"Have courage! You're doing well and what you're going through is not for nothing. It has a function in a larger context, which you can't fully comprehend. We mean well and are not out to burden you with a tough destiny. You are one of us and it is valuable that you have a body, through which you can manifest. It will be good, trust that. And one day you'll be with us again."

"I can have peace with that, but I am struggling with the fact that I feel obliged to live on, while he is in this realm. I am angry. Hermod and I have been together so briefly in this lifetime."

In answer to this they show me a wider perspective, which seems to be a course of several lifetimes, which I have seen glimpses of before, from the perspective of several dimensions. Hermod and I are standing beside each other while images are flowing by. Is this us?

Lives are unfolding before our eyes, passing by like beads on a string called time. Images of lives with and without each other. We see the development of our souls throughout time. The development in this life and what we are going through now by living together in different dimensions, form a preparation for and are part of another reality.

They confirm our love and show me that we shall be together again and, from a wider perspective, we are together now. I should not deny this. I can live from a wider perspective. We experience time as being linear, which is an illusion. All these lives are an expression of one reality.

He is standing there radiantly, proud of me. I am still feeling sad, but also grateful. I know they are right, I often feel this, but as is often the case, my emotions are not in harmony with this insight. I am aware of their respect and my respect for them is deep.

"Have courage!" they say once more.

He takes me back. We also have respect for each other as souls. This has always been a strong point in our relationship. On top of that we are partners. I am also proud of him.

A few days later I am at the beach on my own. The children are with my mother. I swim in the North Sea for the first time this spring and enjoy it, but I am shivering with cold. I remember the clear warm water in Jamaica.

While sitting on the beach I sink into meditation. There is a strong pain. I feel him nearby and tell him I really think the pain is unbearable. He feels my pain. Once more I feel rebellious towards life.

I have tried to to visualise the most wonderful future. And I am trusting that this life could become very beautiful again. I know how beautiful life can be, and I am not afraid of life. But there is nothing that attracts me personally any more. My deepest longing is to be with him... in timelesness.

There is enough to learn in those realms and there are tasks to be fulfilled as well. My motivation to stay comes from the responsibility I feel to be there for the children and for others. I want to be there for them, but this other longing comes from so deep. It is not only a longing for him, it is part of an existential longing to be permanently in freedom and unity. Something we have touched upon in being together. This personal love points towards universal love. This experience of two united souls points towards universal unity.

I walk along the pier. He is walking beside me and the friends are with him. It is a comic perception to walk here in the middle of a group of souls, while the fishermen and other passersby can see only me.

We discuss my task in life. "If you can show me that I still have a task here, I am willing to go for this. I ask for guidance."

"You'll get it. Stay alert. Your path will unfold."

In silence we walk further. It is a pleasant and meaningful communion.

My rebellion melts away.

7

Beyond

How can I stay
in the world of man?
Now I've experienced eternity
in the meeting
of our eyes
the touching of our hearts
the melting of our souls
united Beyond

How can I stay
in this body?
While you have none
How can I stay
between those walls?
-called our 3-dimensional world-
While I pass through
any moment of silence
to be with you

The answer, the only answer
lies in being
Being here and now
is being Beyond.

June

I still dream of him almost every night. My dreams are totally different from my meditations. The meditations feel more real than ordinary reality, my dreams feel less real. However both cast light on different aspects of my consciousness. In my dreams all kinds of conscious and unconscious fragments express themselves in peculiar constellations. Soon after the accident I dreamed a lot about the accident, about his death and all kinds of ways of dying. I my dreams, my love brought him back to life again and our mutual love brought others back to life.

I also had dreams that we were together and had a destination together. I dreamed that he made a meaningful and important piece of art, with which he graduated from the school of life. I dreamed of a hike or a quest, where he led me and the children through the wilderness. I dreamed that we were living on the bottom of the sea as king and queen of the ocean and we had the task of protecting the marine life and the coral reef.

Sometime later I dreamed that I was dying, transcending and joining him. I have dreamed all kinds of things. Gradually the nature of my dreams began to change. They become more real and more like meditations. Sometimes he would repeat and emphasize in my dreams what he has said in meditation. Regularly I wake up with the feeling that I have been in his realm and that we are learning together, although I can only recall glimpses of this. A few times I dream that we are travelling through the kingdoms of nature accompanied by one of my guides.

There is so much happening inside, every week seems like a year. I feel old. On the outside I am functioning quite well. I am there for the children and I am able to open my heart for them and to enjoy this. Fulfilment lies in small things. I am working less and enjoying this too. The household is sort of managing itself. I am working and I have even taught a seminar.

But inside there is resistance to life, about which I feel guilty. I am getting more and more exhausted and I feel sick.

Two participants of my groups offer to give me some treatments. I accept their offer, but I realize I am not even sure whether I want to get better. Yet the treatments and the care benefit me.

One day I discover a lump in my left breast. It's probably my imagination, I think. A little later I find lumps in my left armpit and the lymph nodes are swollen and feel painful. Of course I think what every woman would think at such a moment, but it does not scare me. On the contrary, I feel a surrender to an eventual death. Do I feel the same surrender towards life? No. I feel guilty towards the children.

I decide to wait a little bit before going to the doctor until I have more clarity about my motivation, or rather, my lack of motivation to live. There could be a relationship between these phenomena.

I imagine what it would be like if I were to know that I had only two months to live. I would wish to be fully present, focus totally on the children, be with friends and the people I love and continue writing. Is this different from what I would do if I assume that I have another 40, 50, 60 years to live? No, not essentially.

I realize that my time frame is limited. I want to be with my love, in the stream of love we have experienced together. I want this now. Like a child who has lost her teddy bear and wants it back now. I want to see my needs fulfilled. Despite all my experiences with him in timelessness, despite the intensity of the love I am able to experience now, I am not living accordingly. I have experienced unity, but in daily life I am still living in duality.

I imagine what it would be like to see the children from the other side, witnessing and experiencing their pain. I do not want them to have any pain! I want to live for them. I imagine what it would have been like if I had been under that car, instead of him. This would have been more likely, for he always was more alert and careful in traffic than I am. His decision to run and my decision to step back was a sudden hunch. I recall all the details of the accident. I imagine myself running in front of the car, feeling the smash, the tearing, hearing his scream, feeling myself leaving my body, seeing him sitting on the street with my body in his arms... my devastation, acceptance and freedom, his pain and despair... It is not difficult to imagine, for we were so connected, in a way I was aware of his feelings simultaneously with my own. I realize I would not be able to bear to see him suffering as he has seen me suffer. I would stay with him, as he has stayed with me. He was the one who never really wanted to live, until the last phase of his life. I was the one who wanted to live. If I had died, instead of him, just when he had learned to trust love and life, that would have been unbearable indeed. How would he ever have been able to carry that?

This reminds me of his words, almost a year ago now:

"Don't you know yet what you mean to me? You mean everything to me! You're what keeps me going!"

I had better want to live for him than to die for him.

When I think of others, I feel that I want to live, but do I want to live for myself as well? I do not feel this yet.

There is another seminar on schedule. It is part of a two-year course I teach. I know the participants and usually I really enjoy this work. But the lumps are spreading, They have appeared in my groin as well, big and hard like glass balls. I have pain and I am tired, tired, tired. On top of everything I get flu and the day before the seminar I am in bed with a fever. Now I still have the chance to cancel and postpone the course. I hesitate.

My motivation to teach would be to benefit the participants. I do not have anything to win or to lose. I earn money by teaching, but the money would come anyway at a later time. I could get more ill, but I do not care. In this choice lies an analogy with my choice for life. In life I also have the feeling that there is nothing to win or to lose any more and my motivation to live comes from wanting to be there for others.

Let's go for it! Life as well as the seminar could be beyond my imagination.

After the first day of the seminar the symptoms of the flu disappear like snow in the sun. I feel better and the course is running fine. Hermod is often present and his love surrounds me. Some participants can perceive him as well. One of the themes during these days is the subject of life and death and terminal care. Never before have I been so inspired while conducting a seminar. It is beyond my imagination and I make a breakthrough.

Life can be the same!

After the seminar I go to see my physician, who refers me directly to the hospital for a blood test and scan. I have a week spent in uncertainty while I work on my will to live. Then the results are known: anaemia. That is causing the tiredness. Possibly I've been getting insufficient nutrition during the past months. I am given some medication with iron which will be absorbed quickly. Nobody can tell me where the lumps are coming from.

I am alive and reasonably healthy and I could have a long life ahead of me. I want to know the truth about my unconscious wishes, rather than clinging forcefully to my resistance against life. I sit down for it.

Hermod pops up and takes me to our house, to make me relax a bit. Each time it is lovely to be home. After resting he accompanies me to the light, where he leaves me alone. It is less intense than before, but I experience more clarity inside. I lay out my questions:

"What are my resistances against life?"

The answer emerges in my mind, it seems to be coming straight from my own soul, enlightened by the light. It does not matter, maybe at some point there is no difference between personal and universal knowing.

"It derives out of fear. You have come into life out of love and you had the courage to choose for love, to give and to receive. But now you cannot trust that this love is still present and will be present. You cannot surrender to life in love and unity. You rebel against the resistance you meet in the three dimensional world. You use too much your

personal will, instead of your receptivity and thus you sometimes miss the connection with the environment and with your self."

"What is my task?"

"To manifest love, light, consciousness, which is not 'doing' but 'being'."

"What did/do I find in being with him, which I don't find within myself?"

"Love. When you can manifest the source of love within yourself, you will be free with and without him."

"Is there enough love for others?"

"It's there. You have never wanted happiness just for yourself alone. You have always given. You can only truly give out of love, when you are whole yourself."

Then Hermod is back and he shows me an experience of timelessness. He pulls me into this knowing. I cannot describe it otherwise. I get his insight.

"There is no time. All time occupies the same space. When we identify with our true self, then we are creating our selves, now. When we focus on our connectedness as souls, now, then we are creating a new life, in which we live in soul connectedness, now. In this way we can be together. And in this way we are making a quantum leap in time, reality and we heal the future in the present."

We see a 'next' life throughout time, in which we are together, it is clear and detailed. We have made a preparation for this in this life and we are preparing this now.

"To surrender to the present is the only way. You can't force yourself out of the present moment. Only in the present moment we can be together. When you turn your back on life, you're turning your back on me."

I know he is right. Only by living to the fullest can I experience him in my heart and we can be together. By not wanting to live, I am denying everything we have been talking about, everything we were committed to when we were both still alive, and what we have experienced afterwards: To go for the essence of life, to experience the timelessness of our love, to transcend duality.

"Love between two souls is the most beautiful love in the universe. Don't worry that something will get lost. The universe knows of our love."

In pure joy we merge.

"Thank you love!"

"I thank you."

I can see this does not only concern the two of us. What we are going through is a universal process. Each of us influences his environment, like a stone thrown into the water that causes ripples to spread out. We have never been together just for the two of us. He indicated this beautifully in the meditation he led in Jamaica, when we focussed on the love between us and let it flow out into the universe. That is how it works with love, it is energy which will never get lost. The only path I can choose is to live this fully, with all the love there is inside. Paradoxically this is the only way to let go of him and to live freely. He has always loved paradoxes, because they show the way beyond duality.

Something occurs to me which he told me once. Just before we came together he had told God that he surrendered: "I am ready. Use me."

Now I say the same.

I am ready and at the same time I am not quite ready. My path continues, there is still a long way to go. The wound is far from healed. Still I feel angry for what has been lost, gratitude for what has been given and what still is. Almost daily anger and acceptance, pain and love, joy and sorrow take turns.

Maybe I can learn to be at the height and the depth simultaneously and experience unity and wholeness in multitude, to be in a state beyond duality, in both our worlds.

On earth things need time to change, to heal and to grow. In life on earth there is time and time does heal wounds. Just knowing is not sufficient. What we know does not manifest instantly, like in the other realm. It takes time and it requires an active attitude as well. We have to align our thinking, feeling and action in order to manifest to the fullest. My strength, everyone's strength lies in being in the present, here and now. In the present everything is contained.

Now I am starting to feel willingness to live this freedom. In this I feel supported by him. He has guided me to the experience of oneness. Now I have to find my own way to express this within earthly duality.

After a couple of weeks the lumps disappear from my breast and lymph nodes and I begin to feel stronger again.

8

Gratitude

Every moment together
- even when spent apart -
has been a gift
and still is,
in timelessness
Your love is carrying me
through life and after
Your lightness
inspiring and uplifting
Your care
nurturing

It is and will be
I am grateful to you
for being there

July

It is summer. I take all three children out for a day individually, just as Hermod and I had agreed on, for as he said: "this individual attention is so important."

One evening we are sitting around the table for dinner and are talking about odds and ends. Suddenly Imre asks: "Did Hermand have his eyes closed or open when he died?"

"His eyes were closed," I reply calmly.

She thinks this through aloud and asks further:

"Was there blood coming out of his head?"

"Yes."

"And was he still together or in pieces?"

"He was still whole."

I explain that bone fractures do not mean that the limbs are broken apart from the body. I remember when I was a child how I wondered how a leg could be broken. Children want a clear and graphic picture. When this can be explained normally, there is nothing lugubrious to them. All three of them come to me regularly, at the most unexpected moments, with detailed questions about him, about the accident. It must be even more unreal to them that he is not here anymore, since they were not there when he died.

Our conversation continues. Tara wonders whether it would have been better if I had never met him, then I would not have gone through such pain and sorrow.

I explain to her the value of love and that I learned such a lot from him. I would not have wanted to miss a moment with him, despite the pain I am going through now. He has enriched my life in all aspects. Yoram emphasises that Hermod became happier in his life as well and that he learned from me too. Before we are ready for our dessert, a lot has been reviewed.

Another time we are on the bicycle. Imre is sitting behind me and joyfully we chat about the birds and butterflies we see along our way. Suddenly she says whole-heartedly: "I miss Hermand. I want to see him! I want to die quickly. Let's die quickly, El, for then at least we'll be together with him. I just can't wait until I die and we are with him!"

"As long as we are not dead yet, but alive, shall we make a wonderful life of it?" I propose.

"Yes," she says contentedly.

And with this the matter seems to be closed for now. Now and then she makes these kind of firm statements, but I don't worry because of the light tone she uses.

I still get lots of mail and phone calls from friends and family around and abroad.

I hear from John, the manager of the guest house in Jamaica, that the driver of the car that knocked Hermod down, was taken to court but set free. I am glad. The man did nothing evil. He may have had his place in a larger context. He was like a catalyst in this event. Possibly this has changed his life as well? We have no insight into why this happened, if there is any reason at all.

The network around Hermod is alive. One day a Dutch friend calls, who knew him for more than 20 years. We only know each other from stories. He wants to come along, to meet me. We meet at my place and talk for the whole evening. Once again it is striking how it clicks with his friends. At a certain point he says:

"Elleke, I know that you know this, but I want it to get through to you more deeply: What you gave to him no one else had been able to do. Never before did I hear him speak about anyone or anything, the way he spoke about you, when I saw him last autumn. He was glowing, his eyes were radiant and for the whole afternoon he was unable to talk about anything other than you. And he said:

'Do you remember that special woman I met three years ago at that conference in Amsterdam whom I thought couldn't be for me, because she was married...? I have her now!' I knew he had found what he had been looking for his whole life."

He is pointing right to my weak spot. I know, but it has to get through to me more deeply. This confirmation from his friends is like balm to the wound of loss, the confirmation that our love had been real.

At the end of the evening he says: "What a lucky bird you are, that you learned to know him! And how glad I am to see that the love was mutual, otherwise my Hermod might have made a wrong choice."

Yes, I think to myself later. It is not only that I had learned to know him, but he allowed me into his heart. I was allowed to know his most beautiful and his darkest sides. That is the greatest gift one can give.

I go to England for a week, to attend a seminar by an American doctor, a colleague and friend from the International

Network of Esoteric Healing. There are several of my friends from abroad. This is a network I had wanted to introduce Hermod to, just as he introduced me to the Scientific and Medical Network. He is very close and a few of my friends, who are psychic, can see him too. When a German friend and colleague treats me, I see Hermod standing beside him as soon as the session begins and they are cooperating. The energy is so strong that I almost faint, but it feels good.

Once I injured my knee from skiing. After Hermod had examined me professionally as a physician, he gave me a powerful healing. I was very touched by that. The power of this healing is of the same kind. Afterwards we evaluate.

My German friend, usually so calm and well-balanced, is visibly touched: "I have seen souls during a healing session often, but never before have I so clearly cooperated with a soul. As soon as I put my hands on your shoulders, a powerful soul came standing beside me and we cooperated, but he guided me. I have done things to you which I have never done before..."

"Well finally you have met Hermod," I say, "I had always thought the two of you would like each other, you match in strength."

When we talk to a mutual friend of ours, he tells her in a mock warning: "Watch out with that woman, she has a ghost with her and as soon as you touch her he takes possession of you!"

"Oh, I saw him," she answers dryly, " but when I treated her, he was quietly standing in a corner and observing, that was okay for me."

Later that day we are asked to work with the same partner once more.

"Do you still dare to?' I ask when he comes to me.

"Yes, I have gathered my courage," he says cheerfully.

Again it is a fantastic session. Hermod is clearly present, visible for both of us, but he does not participate this time.

The seminar and all the healing work have done me good. I

feel confirmed in my decision to try to live in both worlds simultaneously and not to deny either of them.

On my way home I visit Stephen and Linda in London. When Stephen picks me up from the tube station it is as if no time has passed since that evening in February. The season has changed, it is summer now, but it seems like yesterday that we were here. When I arrive at their place, Stephen leaves me alone in my room for a while. It is our bedroom with the skylight and the pink bedding. I place our alarm clock at the head of the bed, take a shower and cry.

We have a lovely time together. Like friends who have known each other for years we talk and talk, it's a warm exchange. Hermod is with us. Stephen tells me how Hermod inspired him, uplifted his life and how he is now trying to integrate the enrichment into his being.

That is essential in a mourning process; the integration of the enrichment brought forth by the connection. Each of us has to achieve this in their own way. When he asks, "What about Elleke?" tears well up again. I am living without any idea or longing for a future. The only thing I can say is that the love, the peace, the space I experience inside is what I have always longed for. I am where I have wanted to be. The experience of love between us has brought me here. And I know this applies to Hermod too. But apart from this there is a wound, and it's hurting so incredibly that this draws all my attention. I am in the middle of a state of incubation. We come to the conclusion that in principle, timelessness and spacelesness apply here as well, if I can be in the here and now where all potential is contained. If I stay in the healing process, ideas will emerge naturally.

At home I am alone for another week, during which I meditate a lot. The silence is deepening, as are the experiences in his dimension. The concept of time fascinates me. Once he had phoned me to read out an inspiring quote:

'One's true age is determined by the moments spent in

timelessness...'

When I am with him there is no experience of time. We build or change something on our 'house', we create what we like and we can play indefinitely. Everything happens in a blink. We can take any shape we like and in the more subtle realms we have no shape at all. We are ageless and are able to see and experience throughout time. But when I come out of meditation, a certain amount of time has passed, half an hour, an hour, one and a half hours. Time passes. When I want to do something, this takes time. And I am getting older.

The accident is almost half a year ago now. He has changed since then, as I have changed since then. We are together in how we are in the present. But for him there is no difference, or rather a different difference, between a second and an eternity. For me there is neither when I am with him, but when I am back with my consciousness into my body, I am more and more amazed about the passing of time during daily events.

I notice that I am in less of a hurry, I experience less stress and I get more things done in a more satisfying way. My time consciousness is changing and the quality of what I am experiencing is improving.

He could not handle time very well. He was always late and he could spend a long time on something without getting anything done. I remember one day he wanted to wrap a present for the children, before we were to have a festive breakfast (it was already about lunch time) and he was going to take me to the airport afterwards. The simple task of wrapping this present took him more than an hour and so I had to take my plane that afternoon without having had any breakfast or lunch. But in the car, on our way to the airport we had such a sparkling exchange, it made up for everything. And the present was heartwarming, a telescope to observe the stars, beautifully wrapped with golden tape around!

He experienced life very intensely and lifted others up with his intensity. Timelesness was his favourite concept. Now I begin to understand more that this could have something do to with the fact that he was so strongly connected with this realm of timelesness. Simply phrased, he was so often with his head in heaven. This is what everyone who knew him says. That is why he could inspire us. He was mentally so bright. A talk with him was always an adventure.

Another fascinating concept is space. In his dimension we can travel through different realms and visit other worlds. We can be where we want to be, everything in an instant. The only limitations are those in our own minds, mainly my mind, for I am the one who is bound to the physical world and therefore questioning all the time what is real.

When I come out of meditation, I have to stand up and move my body in order to get anywhere, even to the toilet. Going to the toilet is a peculiar phenomenon anyway. My body is occupying space and within this space there are organs and other substances which need nutrition and the waste products of this metabolic process are being transported out of this space.

All this does not exist in the other realms. In order to go somewhere we physically move from one place to the other, which takes time and energy. In order to cover longer distances it often takes a special kind of 'energy' called money. All of this seems so laborious to me now.

He loved space and travelling. When he was physically moving he felt he was moving mentally as well, he said. He felt confined within our threedimensional time-space frame and he could make himself angry at the restrictions of gravity and entropy. When he was on the move, he expanded. I have always understood his pain and frustration, but now I am experiencing at a deeper level within my own being where his pain was coming from.

Since I often transcend time together with him, a lot of spontaneous images and insights of the past and the future come up, also outside my meditations.

One afternoon, while quietly sitting in the garden, I spontaneously get memories from the time when I was a baby. I re-experience how awkward it felt in this tiny body which could not do what I wanted. How awkward it felt to be submitted to gravity, which held me tight. How ugly and rough the environment appeared to be. Clearly I see the colours and shapes in my babyroom. And I remember my astonishment at the ugliness when we went outside into town. Compared with the transparent beauty and opalescent colours of the realm I had just come from and which I can visit and inhabit now, there is a lot of ugliness in this world.

Above all I remember how much I felt unseen. I was craving love, the love I remembered from where I had come from. I missed my friends, who are my guides now. I remember how adults made artificial sounds to me, as people do with babies, and how they were talking about me as if I were not present. My parents were kind and I was very much wanted, but they did not see who I really was. My mother, who took daily care of me was and still is a loving woman. Still I felt that she did not see me, she saw a baby body, not the soul.

Apart from this I remember a sadness hanging around her at that time, which I cannot remember from later periods of my childhood.

I discuss my memories with her. She confirms that, although she found me cute and endearing as a little baby, she had no idea what was going on inside me. She started to enjoy motherhood more when I began to communicate more, by smiling, babbling and learning to talk. She also confirmed that in the first year of my life she was not truly happy. She had to get used to being married and the life as a housewife and she missed her work as a schoolteacher.

I remember how my memories and perceptions of the other realms gradually faded away from my consciousness. And how the surrounding world had more and more impact on me and demanded more attention while I grew up. I became a child, my consciousness as a soul was pushed to the background, but as with many people, it never disappeared completely. I always kept some awareness of a deep longing for oneness, for love, for paradise.

A colleague once called this 'divine homesickness'. I think this is an excellent definition. This process of incarnation, birth, growing up, and gradually forgetting and becoming a child, I have observed in my children as well. Now I remember my own process and the pain belonging to this. From my early childhood I have always had flashes of memories of what seem to be past lives.

The incredible difference between my memories of the metaphysical and daily reality in the physical has caused a deep uncertainty in me. An uncertainty about who I really am and what the world is like. An uncertainty I have begun to see through and to dissolve since my experiences of an expanded reality. Like a kaleidoscope I perceive the world in her different dimensions.

The longing for paradise is what Hermod and I shared, as well as our longing for love and unity. More than once we had such an intense meetings of our souls, that I sighed that I wished it could always be like that.

The first time his reaction to this was: "But that's paradise, my love. I didn't know you were also longing for paradise that much!"

It was what brought us to Jamaica, although we were very aware that true paradise, the pearl, can only be found within, in each of us, for we are creating this. Love, freedom and peace are of an inner nature.

He takes me through different realms, each inhabited by souls of similar consciousness. Although these realms are a bit like Earth, different kinds of consciousness are living together there.

What souls learn there is often forgotten once they are born again.

This oblivion is a protection mechanism, as I see it now, in order not to burden and confuse souls with memories of past lives, collective unconsciousness and wider dimensions. The consciousness of a child cannot handle this. A child needs to focus on its body, its physical senses and stimuli from the environment. This process takes enough energy. But this oblivion is a hindrance as well.

There is so much we have to learn again, or actually; remember. That is why it is so important to work on Earth. What souls learn here leaves a lasting impression. This is what Hermod and my guides are trying to convince me of.

I can see the value of our partnership. Through me he experiences my process of transcendence, and he learns from this. Through me he can work. Through him I can experience subtle realms, to a depth I could never have achieved on my own.

I am growing through his lightness. We are growing through our love.

In timelessness, life on earth is like a working day. We kiss each other goodbye, I go to my work here, he goes to his work there, both knowing that we shall see each other in the evening. Besides, we stay connected too, like being connected by a mobile phone.

Everything is relative. By this point I have spent such a lot of time in his dimension, that I feel I need a long walk on the beach to get my feet firmly back on the ground. I call a friend and we go.

I am on the phone with friends and family in Norway frequently, even more during these weeks in preparation for our trip to Norway. The children come back from their holidays and we pack our things into the car. I have mixed feelings about this trip. It will be confronting, painful, but I expect it to be healing too, not only for me and the children, hopefully also for the friends and family we are going to visit. It is obvious to me that we should go now, not later.

It is a long drive to the north of Denmark, but it goes smoothly and we have fun with the four of us in the car. That night we camp near the harbour and early the following morning we take the ferry. We sail for the whole day. This is a new experience for me too, until now I have only flown to Norway. Hermod and I had talked about me and the children coming by car. He would pick us up at the harbour in Oslo. That was the idea for this summer. Now we sail into the Oslo fjord, in the bright sunlight, a backdrop of mountain slopes covered with pine trees, and colourful wooden cottages dotted here and there.

It feels like coming home, but he will not be there waiting for us. Imre is singing so joyfully about how we are on our way to Norway and how it is such a long way, that I can hold back my tears.

Norway, August

Vidar is waiting for us in the harbour with his girlfriend and they take us to his house, where we shall stay for the first days. It is a warm and hospitable welcome. He has a pleasant spacious house, surrounded by a huge garden full of fruit trees, a feast for the children. And I am allowed to cry and creep into his arms when it is necessary. Sometimes it is necessary.

The next day we go with Vidar to the grave where the urn is buried. We meet Knut and Cathrine at the entrance to the graveyard. It is a sunny day and the graveyard is full of flowers. In silence we all walk next to each other until we are standing at his stone. I take the bronze sculpture out of my shoulderbag, the disc with the two streams merging to one and the inscription in his handwriting:

'Jeg ønsker deg fra hjertet alt godt i tidløshet'
Hermod & Elleke

I unwrap the silk cloth and hand the sculpture over to Yoram, who had asked me to allow him to lay it down. Carefully he lies it under a rose bush together with some flowers he has picked. Tara and Imre lay their flowers around it.

We are standing in a semicircle. Hermod is standing in between. I can see him very clearly and feel inside him how unreal this is for him, to watch his stone and to see us and the children, standing together so sadly.

Vidar says: "You can't make me believe that he is under this stone!"

"No, he is standing here between us and he feels as unreal as we do," I answer.

It is nevertheless confronting to face this stone with his name and date of birth and the date of his death. I am crying and because of the overwhelming emotions and my shyness and because there are others around, I am not able to communicate with him. Without looking at him I hear his words in my mind:

"Why are you so sad, when you know I am here?"

I cannot answer. The separation of our worlds is unbearable. I take a step closer to the others and we all embrace.

Still I am glad that the sculpture is lying here now. Something is completed. We wish each other well . It is a goodbye in connectedness, it is duality within oneness. I have the same sculpture at my home. Arm in arm we walk back and stand still at his mother Ellen's grave.

The children and I spend the afternoon with Cathrine in Vigeland park. The children show more interest in the fountain and the playground than in the art, so we have an opportunity to talk.

We see some friends, we spend a day on the beach of a small island in the fjord, and the time is spent as a holiday. In the evenings, when the children are in bed, Vidar, his girlfriend and I sit outside with a glass of wine. It feels so natural, as if we are living just around the corner and are visiting them, and Hermod could be walking up the path any moment, coming home from work.

Vidar is concerned: "As his best friend, I feel obliged to tell you this: It is wonderful that you are still in touch with him and I believe you. If there is anyone who should be capable of coming back here and making contact, it would be him. He was always partly living in that world already. And he often said that when he died, he would stay with us. But you need someone here on earth too. Someone who shares the daily things with you, who holds you and cuddles you. He cannot do this any more."

"Hmm, I have thought and felt this myself too," I agree. "The way we are together now cannot replace a partnership on earth, although sometimes it seems like it. But I trust that in the course of time we'll let go of each other more as I develop an openness to meet someone else someone else and consider the possibility that such a person can possibly come into my life."

"I'll have a serious word with him and tell him that he will have to let you go at some time," Vidar says seriously. "You have to tell me when he is there."

"You can talk to him any time you like," I tell him. "The moment you think of him, you make a connection. For him there is no space, he can be everywhere."

Before we go to bed, we give each other a hug. Hermod joins us and the three of us stand in an embrace.

"He is here now," I whisper.

Vidar smiles and in the air he tenderly strokes him on the cheek: "Hello friend."

We leave for the mountains, to spend a couple of days in the cottage of Jan Marcus and Beate and the nephews. The meeting between the children and the nephews is something Hermod had been looking forward to for a long time, when all 'his' children would play together. They have heard a lot about each other. Now it is happening and I feel his smile around us. After spending the weekend together, they leave for home to go back to work and school. The children and I are invited to stay for a few more days on our own and we go for wonderful hikes. In the evening frisbees fill the air and we play games near the fireplace.

Next we visit Cecilia and Robert her husband and their family, who live in a village in the country, and spend lovely time together. Then we move to the south coast where we are picked up by Knut with a small boat to spend a few days together in the family's summer house, which is picturesquely situated on an isle in a fjord.

This place was his home more than any other place on earth. Last year Knut, Hermod and I were here together. And Hermod and I were imagining how it would be to be here this summer with the children. Hermod was discussing plans with Knut for a boathouse, with extra bedrooms "for when more of us have children..."

Now we imagine how it would have been to be here with Hermod.

For the children it is a true paradise. They like 'Grandpa Knut' very much. They go out for trips with the boat, study jellyfish and starfish and explore the island. In the evenings Knut and I sit near the fireplace and have long and open talks. We share our pain and our love for Hermod, although it is a different pain and a different kind of love.

Every morning I take a swim in the fjord and meditate on the rocks. The silence and the peace of this place are healing. It looks a little bit like our house in his realm, but this is earthly, it is dense matter. The colours and the architecture are different. Our house changes shape and lightness, according to our mood and our focus.

Hermod is clearly present during our stay, although not especially more so than in Holland. Place does not matter that much to him.

As soon as I have the opportunity, I sink into meditation. One time he almost pulls me into meditation, so strong is his energy around me and his longing to be together. I go outside, sit down on the veranda and close my eyes. He is standing in front of me and I am almost crushed by the power of his embrace. My whole body reacts. As the embrace becomes a fusion, we ascend and become more subtle.

I realize we are both growing. The way in which we are together now is riper, deeper, than when we were both alive. It is as if we have been together for a whole lifetime, for lifetimes, which may be so.

He takes me through the realms. With a staggering speed we fly over marvellous transparent landscapes. When we fly above a purple canyon-like area, we come to a stop above a mountaintop. There is a deep silence.

He points around: *"This is our world, our universe, the kingdom of the mind. We can be together here. It is our destination to love and reign in this universe and to radiate out."*

Beyond his words I understand what he means by 'reign'; to master our own mind, to discipline the streams of thoughts and feelings. For the landscapes we see are products of our minds, like everything else in this dimension.

It reminds me of the yoga sutra's of Patanjali*: 'Yoga is to discipline the wave in the mind. Then one dwells in one's true nature.'

Now I experience this principle from within. Timelessly we stay in this essence. Then he says: *"Now you have to go back to the children."*

I look at him in surprise, for the children are still playing quietly inside the house and they do not need me at this moment. *"Yes, you have to go to them right now!"*

At that moment Imre starts to scream for help. Without taking time to return to my body, I plunge back inside my body and stand up to go to her. For a moment I look over my shoulder. He is still standing there. I give him a kiss:

"You were right... as always," and I go inside.

During the last week we stay in a house of some friends of Hermod, on a peninsula in the Oslo fjord, and from there we make some cultural trips and visit some friends. All in all we have a real holiday and we are able to enjoy it.

To Hermod's friends and family it is the completion of a picture to meet the children. They can imagine us as a family now. To me this meeting with his family and friends is confronting and healing. We are in his country, but he is not here any more. It is as if I had to go through this experience once more.

The process is intensified by all the meetings and talking about him with people who loved him too. To me it is also the completion of a picture, so that I can now see different facets of him, which I had come to know before through him from within, as they are now mirrored by others from outside. It is a confirmation of what I knew already and an enrichment, as if pieces come together in a larger context. We all need to integrate him, with our positive and negative feelings and by sharing we support each other a bit on our way. As far as I can see this helps to heal all parties, and him too.

Sometimes I still do the exercise of acceptance and forgiveness with Hermod, in which I share with him all the emotions I come across in myself and I experience emotions in him, of his life and relationships which he still carries with him. He is still processing this life and he is being helped in this by souls in his dimension and by all who love him.

I am also working through my own uncertainties. My main concern is that we shall never know how our life together would have been. Would we have been able to express the love and the potential we felt in a fulfilling and creative life? Would we have been able to overcome the practical obstacles? Would we have had our child? Would we have lived a life in freedom in which each of us could grow and unfold?

Gradually I come to the acceptance that we shall never know. And that it is not relevant.

It was good between us and it still is good. There is someone in this universe whom I fully love and who loves me fully. We are fulfilling our potential now, each of us. Nothing in this universe can be lost. I am grateful.

9

Silence

My heart is still,
filled with the love
of our fused souls
All my longings
come to an end

Heart has become home
gateway to the inner world
Silence inside
and around
the wind
in the trees
birds singing
the music of life

Home, September

It is good to be home again.

Hermod's things which we brought back with us in our packed car have found their place in the house. Just as the memories are finding their place in my psyche.

Neighbours and friends come along and we share our summer experiences. It is a beautiful late summer and we sit outside and have meals together in the garden. The children are relaxed and cheerful and after a quiet last week at home they start school again. Quietly I resume my work.

I feel fit, rested and inside there is some joy in living. It comes purely from within and from nowhere else. Something in me has been healed.

It is like coming from another planet. I feel like a different human being, transformed by all these experiences. First the experience of intense fulfilling love, the surrender to another person, followed by immense shock, pain and being torn apart, to be launched into another state of consciousness, which is still growing and manifesting.

For half a year now I have lived without any idea or longing for the future. I was being pulled away from life and I wanted to die. Now I am back from being away and need to re-orientate completely to life. My life has different values and perspectives now. I would still rather be with him permanently and my sadness and missing him as a partner in life has not disappeared. But some will to live, joy of life has returned and this has come from within me. I have come to the conclusion that the one does not exclude the other, on the contrary. What I experience now seems to be part of our human potential, present in each of us.

The extent to which Hermod and I allowed each other in, when we were living together, is the extent to which we can allow each other in now and are able to sense through and inside the other. This is an incredible resource for both of us. We are only beginning to realize this potential.

If we had continued to live together we might have felt more resistance to one another. We might have been distracted by the more or less trivial things of life. We might have been busy with our work, a house and a household, having a baby, dealing with time, space, gravity and daily hassles, like buying a fridge for example. Besides, until shortly before he died, he had never really wanted to live. He wanted to be where he is now.

Yet finally he had chosen for life, a life together. And so had I. Our life could have been wonderfully beautiful! I would have loved to quarrel a bit about that fridge and other trifles. Seeing him with our baby, struggling with nappies, going through the broken nights and the hassles. Raising the children together, seeing them growing up. Working, creating, playing and travelling, growing old together...

I remember an image I had, when we had just met, an image of me sitting at his side when he is dying. He is lying on his side and I am stroking his face and am fulfilled with love and tenderness. It feels like we have gone through a lot together... a long life. I had always hoped that this image would come true when we were old, with children and grandchildren around us. Only now do I realize that I was sitting at his side when he died, he was lying like that and I was stroking him. And I was filled with this overpowering love and tenderness but also with terror. We have gone through a lot, but it was of an inner nature. It feels as if we have shared a whole life, but in earthly time it was only a few years.

We wanted to go for the essence of life. Now we are dwelling in this essence.

We did not know at that time what we know now. Together we exist in an expanded reality. He is learning through me how to manifest in the physical realm, I am learning through him how to manifest in the 'psychic' realm.

The deepest wish to be with him is not necessarily a desire to die any more. It means being in love, in unity.

I experience a sense that our relationship is changing and becoming less personal. We are not so much Hermod and Elleke, as two souls, who are partners and cooperating, one incarnated and one ex-carnated, connected through love.

The love that is pervading me now, can only be expressed in my way of living. My heart and my senses are wide open.

My task, which I asked my guides about, is clear to me now. And it is not only mine, it is everybody's task, to live out the beauty of the universe and to express this, as much as we can, within the given circumstances. It has to do with a quality of being. The way in which we manifest this is unique for every individual.

In meditation we move on, but it does not take me away any more, because I do not necessarily need to be away any more. He did not want to take me away permanently. He wants to take me with him to be together, to grow together.

We dance through the universe. He wants to show me other realms, other worlds, he wants to play and to let me play in life. What I see and experience is going beyond my imagination all the time, but I tend not to trust.

"Break through your reality frame and open up to a greater reality! It may be beyond your imagination," he then says.

Time and again I stretch out and open up to the possibility that experiences could be beyond my imagination.

In the course of the past half year he has changed a lot. He is not the Hermod I knew in life. Though in some way he is more pure Hermod than ever. He is as I have seen him in our most elated and intimate moments. He resides in more subtle realms, where I can visit him, or he comes to pick me up. Still he is often with me as well and then I see or feel him around. Sometimes he touches me, which still feels very physical and which can startle me, especially when it happens unexpectedly, before I have noticed him around. Sometimes he speaks to me in words, more often we communicate telepathically, which can be easily translated into words. However more often the language is beyond anything like words or mental thoughts. I call it 'communication in seedforms' and this is the most direct and pure form of communication I have experienced.

The clearest communication we have is when I sit down and align myself in meditation. Occasionally he asks me to align for a meditation, because he wants to show me something.

When I meditate for myself, which I do for one to two hours a day, he is sometimes there immediately, but usually I go my own way. I start with a little visualisation to relax and build my concentration. In this visualisation I often go to our home.

Since he first brought me to our house, I have learned to find my own way to it and this is often our meeting point. He knows immediately when I make a connection and often I find him at home. The house is beautiful and we can still change it according to our wishes. I sometimes like to do so, he does not do that so much any more, his interest for those physical shapes has declined. Yet he likes to come here.

As he says: *"It's a symbol and manifestation of our togetherness, a home base in the universe."*

I have found out that the house exists across different realms, it changes quality according to our alignment. When my alignment is not subtle enough, the house is a product of my visualisation and it looks pretty dense. Sometimes too dense for him, and then he is not there. But in this familiar, nurturing environment I can align further. It almost works like an elevator, in which I ascend. The house becomes more transparent and the form disappears. Finally there is only a place of light left, created by the energy of the two of us. We are the house, we are home.

And so I have come to an esoteric understanding of the meaning of a home. A home is basically an extension of ourselves. And in the most subtle realms neither the 'self' nor the home needs a form.

In my process of alignment I can come across him, when I am tuned in to the right 'frequency', to reach him at that moment. Over time I have become better able to move through the different realms on my own and, although we may meet at home or elsewhere, often we each go our own way.

When we are together and embrace there are no bodily limits. We sense our way inside the other, our fields fuse and occupy the same space, like two overlapping slides. This is not much different from when we were living together, we could have this sensation of transparency too.

In this transparency the souls meet. Forms fade away and we become fields of light, fields of consciousness. This experience is so authentic and so filled with love, that each time I am deeply touched and feel that there is nothing more beautiful than this.

This is a meeting of human to human, heart to heart, soul to soul.

Since his energy seems to be of a 'lighter' quality, he pulls me further into the subtle realms. What happens then is different each time and the experience surpasses every possible fantasy. Sometimes he takes me through the realms of forms, which are in esoteric traditions often called the astral realms or dimensions. This consists of several sub-realms, of different degrees of 'density', corresponding with the focus of consciousness of the residents. Souls with the same focus are naturally attracted towards each other and inhabit the same realm. The outer extremes of these realms correspond with what we traditionally call heaven and hell and in between there is every variation of what exists in the human psyche. Ultimately all these realms are an illusion, for they are creations of the human mind.

In the realms where we are travelling there is indescribable beauty. I have only seen glimpses of the 'dense' realms, where there is darkness, pain and suffering, but I know them from a deep knowing. We travel through landscapes, which appear like nature in its most wonderful expression, but more majestic, transparent and fluid than on earth, with forms beyond our understanding. Some of these landscapes have come into existence by our togetherness and our play. Here we are mainly just the two of us in our shared reality, like two children in paradise. Other landscapes seem to be shaped by collective consciousness or unconsciousness of mankind and we travel through these realities shared by other souls. In some realms there are souls living more or less like on earth, and many of them are not aware of a greater reality.

All forms are fluid and volatile, yet they are real to those who reside here. For example, when they think that the substance which surrounds them is solid, it is solid and they cannot penetrate it. When they think they have to climb to a mountain top, they have to climb, not knowing that they can think themselves to the top in an instant. Existence in this realm is as tough or as light as they imagine it to be. In these realms of the psyche, emotions and thoughts manifest directly into forms. As long as one is unaware of this process one remains captive in a self-created illusion, whether painful or not. Once one is conscious of one's own capacity of choice and free will, one can create consciously. Many souls are residing in a self-created world and remain there, unaware of the infinite possibilities. There are large groups of souls who have built entire communities, cities, nations and who stay in this bulwark of illusion for an eternity, just as people on earth may live in an illusion for incarnation after incarnation.

Travelling through those realms made me reflect on life on earth. Basically the same principles apply to life on earth. That is why the Buddhist tradition says that life is an illusion, from which one can wake up. In life on earth, emotions and thoughts do not manifest directly into matter, but indirectly, by action, over time. Because of the resistence of matter in the three-dimensional world, we have to act within time and space in order to materialise our thoughts and feelings, so the links between our inner and outer reality are more complicated. But here it is true that many people are not aware of their capacity to create their reality and to give shape to their lives with consciously focussed will, thoughts and directed actions.

The realms of forms are created by souls who are out of incarnation as well as by us, who are living on earth.

All our feelings, thoughts and actions bring about forms in these realms. Loving, joyful, and constructive thoughts produce beautiful, clear, transparent forms. Hermod says, for example, that my loving thoughts of him are like tender strokes and caresses to him, while angry, violent, hateful, fearful, reproachful, insulting, negatively critical and destructive thoughts produce ugly, dark, obscure and dense forms. Fear is one of the main diseases of mankind and our collective fear is visible in the subtle realm as a dark, dense mist around our planet. These forms have an existence of their own and create other forms in other realms as well as events on earth.

Most of us see no correlation between the conditions of our minds and our surroundings. The creative force of our thoughts, feelings and actions like a pebble thrown in a pond, sends ripples out in all directions with corresponding consequences. In esoteric language this is often called the law of karma.

The simplistic explanation of karma is that it is cause and effect. Energy can not get lost and the fruits of all our thoughts, feelings and actions will come back to us one day, for better and for worse. To some this seems to be a fatalistic view, suggesting that everything in our lives is predetermined. To others it implies that we have total control of our destiny and are responsible for everything that happens to us.

In my understanding karma is much more complex than that. Reality in this world is a collective as well as an individual construct. We can determine what is real and meaningful to us and we can choose our reactions to our circumstances. However, it is too glib to say that everyone can choose their thoughts and reactions, for choice implies freedom and awareness of optional possibilities. What of the child soldiers in Africa, brutalised by violence, the street children in Latin America, lured into drug taking and crime, or the victims of sexial abuse made to feel unclean and unworthy by religion and culture? What are their optional possibilities? We cannot call them individually responsible for their reactions to their situation, it is part of a collective responsibility.

And each of us has the responsibility of choice how to deal with these current circumstances. What is our attitude? Do we accept the suffering of others as their 'destiny', which happens to be different from our own? Or do we take shared responsibility for our collective creation? There are no simple answers and the concept of karma should never be used as a substitute for compassionate action.

We are all linked in a multidimensional web and our thoughts, feelings and actions in this world are influenced by and have effects in other realms of existence, other incarnations, other times. It may happen all at once, but since our consciousness is focussed within this time-space continuum, we may experience the results in what we call the future. Since the underlying reality is timeless, it is perhaps more useful to think not of cause and effect but of a sort of 'resonance' between different states.

In these different states the experience of reality can be very different from one another. What is generally considered to be important on this planet – social status, recognition, wealth, personal belongings – is completely meaningless in the subtle realms. Because there everyone can have whatever one can imagine. But what every human being is longing for in the depth of his heart, love, joy, fulfilment and compassion, are permanent qualities, lasting throughout the subtle realms and building constructive forms of beauty.

It is not only that we create forms in the subtle realms, we also live within these forms, they are part of us. It is a kind of primeval soup. And we have the potential to cook a meal from this soup. We have the potential to create something out of this psychic protoplasm, or rather: co-create. Hermod has a strong preference for this last term. Each time I want to use the word create, he corrects me and says: *"co-create!"*. And indeed it adds a significant nuance, for we are not almighty. We work with matter and within matter, but under certain natural laws and circumstances which are created collectively.

Gradually, the more the will, thoughts and actions are aligned with the intention of the soul, whose keyword is love, the stronger is the life force behind it and the more this coincides with a stream of life, through which the circumstances seem to cooperate. This is how we become more consciously co-creative and possibly this is how we individually and collectively may change our circumstances.

From the perspective of the subtle realms, this is a realistic potential, manifesting right now, the very moment we choose to. But from the exoteric perspective, this evolutionary process may take time, even a long time.

This much has become clear to me; from the perspective of the subtle realms, earthly happiness, success, but also pain and suffering in life, are imbedded in a much wider perspective. I say this not to ignore or to accept the suffering, the principle of individual and collective responsibility applies, and we can make different choices as a global community, I say this just to acknowledge that we don't understand what it really is about.

I don't think the totality of implications of this law of karma can be fully embraced by our human mind. The dimension of the soul in all its aspects is infinitely more expanded than our consciousness as a personality. Though we may catch glimpses with our intuition.

We have come across other worlds, I suspect other life forms on other planets. Whether these exist in the physical dimension, I do not know, but in any case they exist in the astral sphere. There are transparent cities, like refined crystal buildings in surrealistic shapes, with a violet glow, where beings live in societies with totally different norms and values and a refined telepathic communication, in which everyone's emotions and thoughts are of a public nature. Lying does not exist, for there is only transparency. Nor does selfish or violent behaviour at the cost of others exist, for every soul is aware of the interconnectedness, and harming one means harming everyone, benefitting one, means benefitting all.

At first this total transparency and 'group consciousness' made me feel very uncertain, but it soon became clear to me that basic moral principles on earth are universal. When the intention is pure, and not directed only towards the separate self, and when feelings, thoughts and will are aligned, there is nothing to fear.

Travelling within one realm feels like a horizontal movement. We move by our will, by changing our focus. In the beginning I often got stuck in this. Using the will is very delicate, it is a subtle mixture of will and surrender. It is not a will-to-control, it is not a will based on fear or distrust, it is not an 'I want'. It is a will deriving from a sincere longing to learn to know the unknown, to learn to know oneself, one's soul, the universe, without being afraid of what one may come across. It is openness to experience. It is a mixture of will and surrender to the unknown. It is the 'wonder state' Hermod spoke about.

When we move through different realms, we make a vertical movement, we ascend, so to speak. This happens by intensifying the concentration or focus, by which the 'frequency' of consciousness is accelerated and becomes more subtle. Here too, the purity of the intention determines the quality of the experience.

When one develops conscious discipline of thoughts and emotions in the astral realm, one works in the mental realm, which is more abstract, clear and real.

In this realm conscious thoughts are generated directly by the soul. The dimension of the soul stretches out beyond this, where consciousness becomes more and more subtle, transcending forms, time and space. Forms are blueprints of light. There are no colours, at least not as we know them, they are more subtle, refined, almost invisible, like a variety of shades of mother-of-pearl, or the nuances of light in a crystal.

I think this realm is what is sometimes called the causal realm in esotericism, and it holds the potential of true co-creation. Here are souls who master the lower realms, where they play and co-create. I use the word play, because everything in this realm is of such a lightness, a totally different quality from the earthly realm, and hence coloured with a touch of humor. It is serious though. In this more subtle realm the blueprints are created which give an outline for the development of the denser realms, including the earth.

On this level communication between souls is pure and direct, beyond all language. It is communication of seed-thoughts and values. Souls recognise each other's consciousness, beyond outer forms and see right to their core. It is not clear to me whether these souls belong or have belonged to any human form at all. Some have, others have not, as far as I can perceive.

Hermod and I recognise each other in our consciousness on this level, without the outer form and personalities we have had in our life. The personalities of Hermod and Elleke are irrelevant here. We are souls and a couple and as such we are connected by love. Besides we are part of a group of souls, who are connected as brothers. Individuality does exist, however, in a rudimentary, pure form.

The unconditional love is disrobed from all coats of the personality. Beyond this realm there is no individuality any more, only grace.

When we accelerate our frequency, we adjourn to the ultimate light, which demands a strong, one-pointed concentration, which I cannot always summon. These are the purest experiences, where we transcend our individuality and our togetherness in a universal experience of oneness, where there is knowing. These experiences are beyond words and beyond my comprehension. The only word coming to my mind is: 'God', but this word too is inadequate. The main difficulty in describing these experiences is that there are simply no words for them.

Experiences like these are transforming. Afterwards I am not the same person as before. Many spontaneous insights emerge and a deep inner peace sinks into me. But the more I see and experience, the more I realize how little I know, how very little I am able to take in of what exists in reality, and above all, how pathetically little I am able to manifest of this beauty. What remains is awe and humility.

Where is this going to? I often wonder. How far can this continue?

"Into infinity," he answers joyfully. "There are no limits, but worlds beyond worlds, with forms of consciousness of which you have no idea yet. Don't worry, we aren't in a hurry, there is no time. We can take it easy and explore and experience."

He is in his element. This is Hermod at his best. He travels around and feels at home everywhere, just as he did in earthly life. The ease with which he moves through the realms is not that common, as far as I can see. It requires an expanded consciousness, the ability to direct and hold the attention purposefully, a great flexibility and the capacity to accelerate and slow down one's own frequency. I realize once more that he is an advanced soul, a realisation that came to me regularly when we were both living. I was touched by his purity then and I still am.

We study life and continue our quest for the essence of life, or right now it would be more appropriate to say: existence. All journeys through the realms are part of this study, which is a healing process for both of us. To me it is a challenge to manifest this consciousness in life, to experience oneness in daily activities, in my work, in my contact with people.

To him it is an integration and processing of the life that has been with the other aspects of his being that are parts of him in other realities. The integration and processing also happens through his connectedness with those with whom he has been affiliated. By being with us he learns from life by experiencing it from the viewpoint of the other side. In this process he gets guidance from other souls and he receives a kind of education. This is a rather usual phase for souls who have just passed, to spend 'some time' (according to our earthly time reference this can vary from a couple of days to a couple of hundred years) close to the earthly realm in order to learn and to support beloved ones. Although in some cases this is not conscious and it happens that souls cannot let go of the earthly realm and cannot accept that they have passed. Some are not even aware that they have died.

Because Hermod is also conscious in more subtle realms, he can move his consciousness with ease. And sometimes I perceive him as the man whom I have known, with all his sunny and shadow sides, but more often I perceive him as soul, in which several personalities are integrated; and sometimes I perceive him as pure consciousness beyond all personal traits. I do not understand this completely. It seems to be according to the 'frequency' at which he is focussed and/or where I am at that moment.

One of his tasks is 'awakening souls', as he calls it himself. He accompanies other souls in their liberation and helps them to break through their emotional and mental limitations and experience themselves in their essence. A group of souls cooperate in this work. When I become aware of this, it reminds me of Stephen's words in his letter to Knut; that Hermod was not only a doctor of bodies, also a doctor of souls. He still is.

But as far as I can see, he carries out this task on a subtle level, which is not apparent yet in our time consciousness. It takes place in several realities, which all are part of the being whom we call Hermod, who is integrating these different aspects of his being into one.

One evening I sit down and he is standing before me. I do not feel too well, my period is about to break through and the hormones are bothering me. On top of that my skin is irritated and my hair needs to be cut. Normally I would want to freshen myself up if he were to be here physically, or if I were expecting a visit from anyone at all. I would not show myself to anyone like this. Because he is there so clearly, I am very aware of this. Once more it is rather a comic situation.

"I am not in a state to be looked at!" I say uncomfortably, but with a smile.

He is looking straight through me.

"You don't know how I see you," he answers tenderly and seriously. "To me you are the most wonderful and beautiful being!"

At that very moment he pulls me into his experience, and I experience through him how he perceives me. I see myself as a magnificent, radiant, transparent being, radiating love, dignity and knowing. I recognise my essence, it's similar to his. For a timeless moment we stand facing each other in a flow of love.

Then he takes me into another experience. From his perspective I see myself in my daily consciousness, preoccupied with daily hassles and activities, varying from cleaning the toilet, shopping, cycling the children to school, to cuddling them, talking to friends, teaching, having sessions with clients, writing and meditating.

I see how he stays in his perception of my essence, while I lose this consciousness throughout the day, and most of the time I am able to manifest very little of this essence. Like an EEG scan I see the quality of my consciousness going up and down throughout the daily flux of activities.

His perception is without judgement, but I am ashamed. I thought I was reasonably focussed. Yet, from the viewpoint of timelessness, the moments in which I am in this state of consciousness are like drops in the ocean. Even in my meditations, my consciousness flickers like a candle in the wind in my attempts to comprehend what he lets me experience. How patient he is with me, in taking me by the hand time and again and being there for me. And how patient my friends are!

He smiles: *"Don't let yourself be scared off. You know how little of this essence I have manifested in my life and how you have lifted me up. You're doing amazingly well in how you're able to come with me and how you lead your life. My patience means nothing in timelesness, it's no effort. Besides, your love for me is so nurturing, you have no idea!"*

In a flash I experience through him the continuous stream of love, flowing from me to him on a subtle level, and through this he is confirmed in his essence and hence being supported on his way. That is the universal power of love.

"But I want to stay in this essence consciously, I want to stay in this love and radiate it out. It is ridiculous that I lose it time and again every day, while this is who I truly am! And I know it, I've always known it and often enough I've caught glimpses of it. Why lose it? I want to live in this!"

I feel a growing rage inside. A rage which I recognise from him. I am talking, like he did, when he was frustrated about his limitations and about life.

Then he shows me the consciousness of humankind in all her qualities, like gradations of light. We see the suffering all over the world, the pain, the fear, the grief, the violence. Primary and fierce in areas of war, famine and disaster, more subtle, yet just as destructive in societies like ours: destructive thoughts, egocentric thoughts, greed, perverted activity, inertia, numbness and a lot of self-intoxication with stimuli, like TV, sound, computers, traffic noise. It is a real cacophony of thoughts and impressions in the human psyche.

There is little manifestation of the cosmic potential, the potential of the soul of each human being. We watch in silence with sadness in our hearts. I see into his heart and see the pain, which he carried in his life, so strong that it could paralyse him. Still in this wide overview there are also human feelings of joy, love and compassion sparkling like stars in a dark night, with here and there even a shining solar system. We see how human consciousness is continuous throughout the dimensions, becoming brighter and radiant, less obscure and more essential, until it fuses with cosmic unity. In the course of time this may manifest.

We are standing in our lightbodies in each other's arms.

"You see, you're not doing so bad. There is still a lot of work to be done on earth," he finally says softly.

I lay my head against his breast. There is nothing that I want, nothing, only silence, this love and this unity.

At the same time I feel I want to manifest this and contribute something to the manifestation on earth in my own limited way. I want this peace for everybody! I remember our talk, on the last day of our life together, at the terrace on the beach, when he spoke about the timelessness of our love and the experience of paradise and how furiously he added that he wanted everyone to experience paradise!

He knows what I am thinking, I know that he knows. We do not need to say anything anymore.

10

Freedom

The art of living,
is to dance
to play
to create
to go
beyond imagination
The doors are open
path to the unknown
unfolding
The choice
to live
in freedom
is to each of us

October

I would rather stay in the realms of causality and oneness. There is something transforming in every experience and after each experience I have become a slightly different person. The challenge lies in living this new expanded reality. I have changed, my outlook on life has changed, and hence my life is supposed to change. But how?

Where do I go from here?

My life seems to be blank. I am still in a sort of incubation phase. But I know there will come a time of letting go and finding a new relation to the world and to myself.

In order to develop a way of life that's appropriate to my present expanded reality I try to follow my heart, my intuition, and my intellect as well. That is a lot to integrate, the complexity of being human. It requires alignment and focus. Rest and space are needed. I create this by working little and spending a lot of time in meditation, in timelessness. I am coming down to earth, by trying to live quietly. The exercise is not to doubt, not to be uncertain, not to judge, and not to submit to negative thoughts and feelings. In practising this, thinking, feeling and acting become aligned and the experience of oneness is more likely to be maintained. Oneness makes life simple.

When I become distracted by what he calls 'the more trivial things of life', I get split. Then I often hear him clearly in my mind, sometimes with a joke, or sweet remark, and mostly with the message:

"Don't negate yourself. Live your love. Live your truth!"

Daily practicalities of earthly life, like running the household, tasks of motherly care, administrative hassles, which can be so demanding in our modern society, are running more smoothly than ever before. Maybe because I am not bothered by them. Problems seem to resolve themselves.

Although at times I have the feeling that I am floating around my body instead of being in it, and I perceive the world from a different angle. This is handy when the children's hamsters have escaped and need to be found, but overall it is hard and requires my concentration to coordinate. By physical exercise and healthy food I am trying to maintain consciousness of my body. And of course the children are very important in my life. What needs to be done after I have been in different realms? Cuddling the children, feeding them and washing the dishes. They keep me grounded and draw me into their world with their sweet, funny, sad and nasty commonplace things. We are a good team together.

The space which is developing within me, I also create around me. I make some changes in the house and in my practice. I redecorate, paint, do some odd jobs and create a new atmosphere. This is nurturing for me and for others as well. My work as a psychologist consists of creating space for others, being there for others.

My experiences in the subtle realms make me curious. I am well aware that I am not the only one who has experiences in other dimensions. And I want to have more insight into this reality and communicate with others about it. However these experiences cannot be shared with everyone and I do not know yet how to talk about it.

I follow the debate about the nature of consciousness in the periodical of the Scientific and Medical Network. Via Hermod I have become a member of this Network. It is one of the many things he left to me. Before he came into my life I was already interested in the relation between science and subjective experiences of reality and spirituality. The Network is committed to open exploration in science and human experience. It has no corporate views but questions the materialistic and reductionist assumptions which tend to underlie orthodox science.

In the periodical I come across articles on mystical and near-death experiences written by scientists, like Peter Fenwick* and Melvin Morse* and it seems that, although it is agreed that specific areas of the brain are involved in these experiences, many now question the assumption that the brain actually generates consciousness.

It could be that brain interacts with consciousness to create our individual experience, but in certain altered states we reach beyond the personal and experience a taste of an underlying reality which is timeless, spaceless. It maybe that healers can access this underlying reality in their work. My experiences are consistent with this view and similar to many other mystical experiences reported in the literature and I get goosebumps of recognition.

I am intrigued by all this and decide to explore the connections which the Network facilitates. Shortly after I have decided this I get a letter from Diana, a member of the Network, and I am invited to speak about my experiences with Hermod in this expanded reality and to get in touch with some scientists who carry out research on the topic. This is a line I want to follow, a line which challenges me to carry on and to explore other dimensions of life and beyond.

All my experiences I have always considered to be my subjective reality and not necessarily part of someone else's reality. I have considered them as my personal inner world and choose to explore this. Often I have wondered what is imagination and what is real. Hermod's answer to this is known by now:

"We are co-creating our own reality with our imagination!"

This corresponds with Buddhist teachings, with the philosophy of classical yoga and with the experiences of mystics throughout history and in different cultures and even with some psychological schools and hypotheses in post-modern science.

Curiosity is tickling me. I want to go beyond the self-created limitations of my mind, to explore beyond my imagination. I want to grow.

This is linked with Hermod's ideas about expressive art and his connections in the world of expressive art therapy. After his training in medicine, when he was working as a physician, he studied psychodrama and subsequently participated in several courses in expressive art therapy. To him this was healing, a quest of the soul for expression in life.

We compared my work with meditation with his creative art. Both have to do with the exploration of a subjective reality, a personal inner world in order to express an inner esence, beauty. We saw a mutual fruitfulness and stimulated and inspired each other. We wanted to act this out in our 'wonder workshops'.

Before I met him I had been creative in several ways, but I always kept it just for myself. He encouraged me to step out, not to be afraid to express myself in dance, movement, writing and poetry. We had ideas to attend a course together this summer. Now I get information about this education via his friends and it is uplifting. Maybe one day I shall treat myself to such a study. It is another thread in my life which continues and which motivates me.

By putting words to my experiences in writing, they become more substantial. And by writing I dwell in a creative stream of life. He made me see art as an expression of the soul, to express the inexpressible in creation, to play with imagination and reality, to go beyond. Art is connected to love. Art is creation and a free creation can only evolve out of love, when imagination can find expression in acceptance. Through him I have come to see love as an answer from the soul to life. Thus the pattern of my life is woven from different threads, which are each essential to me to carry on and to choose a direction for my new relation with the world.

I go to my work room, sit down and align.

We meet and ascend together.

Hand in hand (but without form) we are standing in the light.

A deafening silence and void.

In front of us there are golden gates, opening, and behind a magnificent, transparent, opalescent world stretches out. There is vast space, a deafening silence and light, no manifestation of form. A universe beyond a universe.

In wonder we enter. There is a knowing throughout time and infinite worlds. We see our destination like a red thread, which we can give shape with our creative potential. In this we take part in a universal plan, stretching out beyond our comprehension.

We have entered a dimension that is new to me, beyond unity and light, which until now, I considered as the ultimate. Yet it feels like coming home. It is more real than reality. There are no forms, only consciousness.

Although they are invisible to me, there are other beings around, who reside here permanently. They give signs of appreciation and recognition. I know they see into every vessel of my being, with all my limitations, which makes me feel very humble. I experience them as beings of pure consciousness, vast, clear, endlessly wise and knowing and filled with unconditional love. It is not possible for me to communicate with them. I experience everything as being veiled. I am not ready yet and there are no words for this. The frequency is so high, it is almost unbearable to me. I tend to fade away.

He looks at me: *"Be free with me. This is infinite."*

I feel I am longing for nothing other than to explore this, to be this, to manifest this inexpressible experience. We are one in this longing. But it requires such an alignment to be here. It requires a totally different way of being, total acceptance, surrender, commitment to this journey, and to be of service to a plan which is beyond my personal will and understanding. It goes further than I could ever imagine. It also requires me to let go of him as a person, for in this realm the personal is irrelevant.

"Yes, I wish to," I choose. Then I fade.

He accompanies me to less subtle realms. With the greatest effort I return to my body. My heart is aching.

When I come out of my meditation and I am back in daily reality, I wonder what this choice will bring me. At times I am being torn by the pain of longing for this unity and by being confronted by duality.

Can I go on into infinity? Do I trust the universe, stretching out so far beyond my personal 'I'? Am I not submitting too much to this expanded reality? Is it possible to integrate both realities in life? Can unity be experienced within duality at all? And finally: am I able to let go of him? All this is questioned by the sceptical voice of my mind.

Together we wanted to go for the essence of life. Since his passing he has taken me with him, further into other realms, closer to the essence. Time and again I have chosen to go for my reality and to let go of my doubts. My motivation to do so has of course been influenced by my grief and my longing for him. The experience has helped me to bear the pain, it has brought me back to a willingness to carry on and it has given me inspiration to live a fruitful life, for others and for myself. There is common ground between my experiences and science which I would like to investigate and which I would like to contribute to. I want to be creative. I want to be innerly free and to share this freedom.

The line is continuing. It is not just a passing whim as a result of grief. It goes beyond. It is not only about Hermod and me, it is about a fundamental choice to live in an expanded consciousness.

It is a theme of life, it has always been a theme of my life, of his life, of both our lives together, and it is still a theme of my life.

What consequences does this have?

I sit down and present this question to him.

"Our journey continues, as long as you want. There is still so much I want to show you. But to continue you need to surrender and this will be expressed in your life in a way beyond your imagination."

I see a crystal line.

"It is unmistakable. I wish nothing other than to explore this reality, obtain insight, live it, express it and contribute as far as my capacity permits. This is what I have always wanted... But what about us? I want to go where you are going and at the same time I am sometimes afraid that this will hinder my life as well as yours and then I think I have to let go of you."

"We each have our own path and we can never follow each other's path, not in life and not beyond. But we can share part of our reality and this I want with you."

"I want this too. But how? I am exposed to time, you know, and I may have to go on for a while here on earth, even though it is only a fraction in timelessness... and I have to go on without you."

"Trust! Acknowledge that we are together here. When you surrender to this expanded reality, you also surrender to life. When you acknowledge the essence of our love, the quality of this love will manifest in your life. We set each other free, although I'll always be

with you and support you and you will be with me. You can let go of me, lead your life and be happy."

It sounds paradoxical, but I get his insight and I now understand that this applies multidimensionally and all this can coexist. I see that we are together in processing our personalities, in our sun and shadow sides, and we support each other. I see that we can let go of each other in the course of time, and we will each grow further. I see my life continuing, and new relationships may develop.

His 'life' is continuing, in realms beyond my reach and in lives where he has other relationships. And I see that in timelessness we are connected as souls. And I see that we are together in other realities and we will be together. I see that we are part of a group of souls, in a realm where personal does not apply any more, where strengths are combined in service of a purpose beyond individual fulfilment.

I feel trust in life, in the laws of the universe. I trust that we each shall grow according to our fullest potential. And I trust that love will remain, not only between the two of us. All love between humans is substantial and and remains permanently in the universe.

We are all present in all realms simultaneously (for there is no time), as human being and as soul. We live on earth with our joy and our sorrow, we reside in denser realms of pain and fear as well as in the beautiful realms of forms, in the subtle realms of causality, and in the realm where there is no individuality, only unity. We are a holographic part of the universe in all aspects, indeed, as described in the Bible, like 'the image of God'.

However for most of us our consciousness is focussed on a tiny particle of the whole. We are condensed in our personalities in the time-space frame of the here and now, with a small time span to the direct past, within the one life time. We think we are this 'I', this person, with these personal traits. This is a part of us, but we are more. We are beautiful multidimensional beings.

I feel free and peaceful. The gates are open. It is the image of the gates and the naked female figure I saw half a year ago in meditation, the image he found so beautiful. I knew then that I would go through the gates towards freedom. Now I am passing through, naked, stripped of defences.

I am allowed to play and life may be beautiful.

Being free does not mean: being free from pain, for pain is inherent in life.

It does not mean: being perfect, for perfection is an illusion.

It does not mean: being unlimited, for in this three-dimensional reality we simply have our limitations.

I think I can accept this now.

"I'll set you free and thus myself. I trust that we set each other free and stay connected as souls in freedom. I have loved you since the first moment I saw you, and actually before that, for I have always known that you exist and I'll always love you. I can see the best way to honour this love is to live it. I move on."

"I love you in timelessness. Your life will change. Be prepared for the unexpected."

We do not say goodbye, for there is no goodbye, but another step on the path to the unknown.

God's love is by its nature warmth. When it lights on someone without any limit, it plunges the soul into ecstasy. That is why the heart of one who has felt it cannot bear to be deprived of it. But he gradually undergoes a strange alteration in proportion to the love that enters into him.

Isaac of Nineveh

In: 'The Wedding Present'

Acknowledgements

As it goes with stories, they are never the creation of one person, but merely the fruit of an interaction between people. So it is with this story.

For the coming about and for all the support and friendship I have received in this period, I would like to thank people.

This story would not have been written without Hermod. In a way it is our book. Thank you for coming into my life. Thank you for being you. 'Takk for alt'!

Yoram, Tara, Imre, you are precious treasures in my life. I hope that later, when we look back to this period, we shall remember the good parts of it as well.

Mum, thanks for your continuous support and concern in all possible ways. You have always been there for me and the children. I have no words for this.

Anja, I'm happy with you, as a sister and best friend.

Knut, Jan Marcus, Cecilie, Cathrine, Christiane, Beate, Robert, and also Knut Johannes, Marcus, Lauritz, 'tusen takk' for the hearty way in which I was received into the family in sunny times. And for the warmth and support and togetherness when life went so different from what we had all hoped for. My thanks as well for your trust. I hope that my story can contribute something for you. A kiss for Axel and Frederik.

Especially I want to thank Joop for your support and coaching in finding my way between heaven and earth. And for your advice, constructive criticism, enthusiasm and dedication to my story.

Peter, thank you for your support in times when it was most difficult.

Beverley, Sybille, Petra, Michiel, and all my friends, thanks for keeping an eye on me.

Vidar, Stephen, Linda, Jørn, Mai-bente, Kristine, Morten, Christian, Gunnar, Peter R., and many others: friendship goes 'beyond'!

Siemen, your sculpture is a key between now and timelessness.

Liset, Lizette, Irene, Marrit, Madelon, Pieter, Bianca, Juliane and all dear people in my groups, our cooperation, your enthusiasm, support and healing have kept me going.

Friends of the INEH, I have felt carried by a fine network of threads of connectedness, all over the planet.

John, thanks for all your support in Negril. You showed me that there will always be love and humanity, even in the midst of chaos and despair.

To all my neighbours, you are as dear to me as far away friends.

Paule and Anke, a special meeting has brought us together, a friendship through which this story has become a book.

And my deepest thanks to Di, for all your dedication to the editorial work of this English version, your enthusiasm and your critical questions. I know it was a lot of work to change my Dutch-English into British-English and I am very grateful for your patience.

And after all: David and all those from the Scientific & Medical Network who were in Jamaica, thanks for the support which I got from many of you afterwards. I see lines which carry on, which can be inspiring and fruitful.

And to you, both David's, my special thanks for your believe in me, your effort and support in having this English version published and all your encouraging words!

Thank you all!

References

Fenwick, P. (1998). How to Understand and Experience Love. Network. The Scientific and Medical Network Review, 68, 2.

Long, M. (1999). The Wedding Present. Riches of Spiritual Wisdom for Life's Journey. Herefordshire: Gracewing, p. 76, 170.

Morse, M. (1998). The Right Temporal Lobe and Associated Limbic Lobe Structures as the Biological Interface with an Interconnected Universe. Network. The Scientific and Medical Network Review, 68, 3-7.

Nhat Hanh, T. (1988). The Heart of Understanding. Berkeley, California: Parallax Press.

Nhat Hanh, T. (1996). Be Still and Know. Reflections from Living Buddha, Living Christ. New York: Riverhead Books.

Pierrakos, E. (1990). The Pathwork of Self-Transformation. Bantam Books. New York.

Pierrakos, E., Saly, J. (1993). Creating Union. The Pathwork of Relationship. Del Mar, California: Pathwork Press.

Pierrakos, E., Thesenga, D. (1993). Fear No Evil. Del Mar, California: Pathwork Press.

Pierrakos, E., Thesenga, D. (1997). Surrender to God Within. Pathwork at the Soul Level. Del Mar, California: Pathwork Press.

Radin, D. (1997). The Conscious Universe. The Scientific Research Of Psychic Phenomena. New York: HarperCollins.

Roads, M. J. (1985). Talking with Nature. H.J. Kramer, Tiburon, California.

Roads, M. J. (1990). Journey into Nature. H.J. Kramer, Tiburon, California.

Roads, M. J. (1994). Journey into Oneness. H.J. Kramer, Tiburon, California.

Roads, M. J. (1995). Into a Timeless Realm. H.J. Kramer, Tiburon,

California.

Sheldrake, R., Fox, M. (1996). Natural Grace. Dialogues on Science & Spirituality. London: Bloomsbury Publishing.

Taimni, I. K., (1961). The Science of Yoga: A Commentary on the Yoga-sutras of Patanjali in the Light of Modern Thought. Madras: Theosophical Publishing House, 1961.

BOOKS

O is a symbol of the world, of oneness and unity. In different cultures it also means the "eye," symbolizing knowledge and insight. We aim to publish books that are accessible, constructive and that challenge accepted opinion, both that of academia and the "moral majority."

Our books are available in all good English language bookstores worldwide. If you don't see the book on the shelves ask the bookstore to order it for you, quoting the ISBN number and title. Alternatively you can order online (all major online retail sites carry our titles) or contact the distributor in the relevant country, listed on the copyright page.

See our website **www.o-books.net** for a full list of over 500 titles, growing by 100 a year.

And tune in to myspiritradio.com for our book review radio show, hosted by June-Elleni Laine, where you can listen to the authors discussing their books.

MySpiritRadio